MYSTICS AND PROPHETS

MARVELS & MYSTERIES

MYSTICS AND PROPHETS

P
·PARRAGON·

This material has previously appeared in
partwork form as *The Unexplained*

Published in 1997 by Parragon
Unit 13-17 Avonbridge Trading Estate,
Atlantic Road, Avonmouth, Bristol BS11 9QD

ISBN 0-75252-187-X

Printed and bound in Italy

CONTENTS

INTRODUCTION

Many, perhaps all of us have at one time or another experienced a moment or two of sudden clarity or insight, times when we felt at one with the world, or had a strong feeling that something was about to happen. However, very few of us can legitimately claim to have a more permanent or ready access to times, realms and beings beyond the understanding of the rest.

This book looks at the lives, works and prophecies of a wide selection of these special people, from the undeniably holy to the relentlessly secular. Many mystics express themselves through established religions; Sai Baba, St Thérèse, Eastern yogis and Christian stigmatics all fit in this category. Others, such as George Gurdjieff and Madame Blavatsky, founded religions – or at least mystical groups – of their own. Wilhelm Reich expressed essentially mystical ideas through the medium of science, while Edgar Cayce used mystical means to inspire visions of a technological future

The gift of prophecy is potentially one of the most useful of all psychic gifts, though more often than not it is a tantalizing one. People who make a profession of prophecy tend to mask their predictions in riddles, as did Nostradamus, or to make them so vague that some event can always be found to fit, as did Joanna Southcott. Some of the most extraordinary prophecies, fulfilled in some detail, have come not from soothsayers, but from ordinary people who have had dreams and visions of great disasters – the sinking of the *Titanic*, the wreck of the *Hindenburg*, the landslip at Aberfan. The terrible paradox of premonitions, though, is that none has ever averted a disaster; it seems that the future, once revealed, is forever fixed.

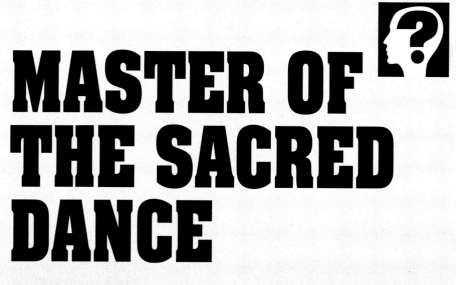

MASTER OF THE SACRED DANCE

George Ivanovich Gurdjieff, left, earned his living as a stage hypnotist, and travelled in search of 'a certain knowledge, of certain powers and possibilities exceeding the ordinary possibilities of Man'. Having apparently found them – although, even to his closest disciples, he would never say where – he put this secret knowledge to use by inventing a philosophical system 'for the harmonious development of Man'. Gurdjieff founded his first institute for tuition in this system in Tiflis, Georgia, below, in 1919.

IN THE 1920S, THERE APPEARED AN OBSCURE ARMENIAN WHO CLAIMED TO BE ABLE TO TEACH A METHOD OF REALISING MANKIND'S HIGHEST POTENTIAL

On 9 January 1923, the New Zealand writer Katherine Mansfield died at the Institute for the Harmonious Development of Man at Fontainebleau, near Paris. She had been fighting a losing battle with tuberculosis for several years. Disillusioned with conventional treatments, she had entered the Institute some weeks before, convinced

The New Zealand writer Katherine Mansfield (1888-1923), *right, became a devotee of Gurdjieff's system through her friend A.R. Orage, below right, editor of the English literary journal* New Age. *Katherine Mansfield died peacefully of tuberculosis at Gurdjieff's Institute for the Harmonious Development of Man at Fontainebleau near Paris. 'One has,' she wrote some weeks before her death, 'the feeling of having been in a wreck and by the mercy of Providence got ashore... It's a real new life'.*

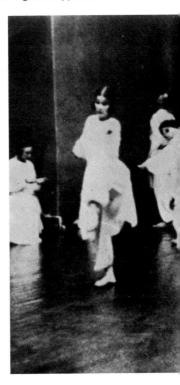

Gurdjieff's philosophical system, upon which his Institute was based, proposed that, ordinarily in Mankind, the physical, emotional and intellectual faculties (which Gurdjieff called 'centres') were unintegrated and out of balance, and Man therefore functioned inefficiently and mechanically. By following a programme of rigorous physical and psychological exercises, Gurdjieff's pupils hoped to develop their centres harmoniously, and eventually to make contact with a source of higher energy that would put them in possession of psychic powers not normally available to Man. As Gurdjieff said in a talk reported by his pupil C.S. Nott, 'directed' attention, in which all three centres – physical, emotional and intellectual – take part, is real concentration: then, 'a man can move a mountain.'

Although Katherine Mansfield died before she had an opportunity to advance in the Gurdjieff system, there is no doubt from her letters that she found peace and happiness in the last weeks of her life at the Institute: 'I believe Mr Gurdjieff is the only person who can help me,' she wrote on 24 October 1922. 'It is a great happiness to be here...

that, by achieving spiritual regeneration, she would also achieve a physical cure for her illness. She wrote to her estranged husband, John Middleton Murry, that she hoped to get 'really cured – not half cured, not cured in my body only and all the rest as ill as ever'. The Institute had only recently opened; and the physical conditions of life there for a tuberculosis patient were hard – it was extremely cold, and all the residents had to engage in strenuous physical work. Nevertheless, Katherine obviously found a great deal of solace in the few weeks she spent there. 'One has,' she wrote in a letter on 20 October 1922 – 10 weeks before her death – 'the feeling of having been in a wreck and by the mercy of Providence got ashore... It's a real new life.'

ARCANE KNOWLEDGE

Katherine's husband and friends were horrified that she had put herself in the hands of the dubious character who ran the Institute. George Ivanovich Gurdjieff was an Armenian Russian, who claimed to have acquired arcane knowledge during prolonged travels in the Middle and Far East. He had run study groups for 'the harmonious development of Man' in the early years of the century in St Petersburg and Moscow, and was trying to establish his first formal Institute in Tiflis when the Russian Revolution forced him to flee and take refuge in France. It was rumoured that a wealthy English Theosophist admirer had provided the funds to purchase the lovely house and grounds of the Prieuré at Fontainebleau, a former Carmelite monastery, where he set up his second Institute. Gurdjieff, at this time, was aged about 50. He was a man of great vitality, who enjoyed good food and company – and was extremely attractive to women. One observer described him as 'altogether Eastern in appearance', with long black moustaches and piercing eyes; Katherine Mansfield said he looked 'exactly like a carpet-dealer from the Tottenham Court Road'.

Such beautiful understanding and sympathy I have never known in the outside world .'

Katherine had heard about Gurdjieff and his Institute through her friend A.R. Orage, editor of the literary journal *New Age*. Orage became Gurdjieff's chief English disciple, and later ran a group of his own in New York.

Other well-known people became Gurdjieff followers during the 1920s and 1930s, including the American architect Frank Lloyd Wright, and Dorothy Caruso, wife of the operatic singer Enrico Caruso.

So how had Gurdjieff arrived at the remarkable philosophical 'system' that had such an influence during this period? It is not easy to determine the facts of his youth and formative years, partly because he himself was apt to give conflicting accounts of his early days to different disciples. It seems probable, however, that he was born in 1872 in Armenia. His father was Greek, his mother Armenian, and he himself had Russian nationality. From an early age, he was fascinated by the occult and magic. He told Peter Ouspensky, his chief Russian disciple, how – as a child – he had come into contact with a group of 'Devil-worshippers', the Yezidis. He had observed, for instance, how a Yezidi boy would find it impossible to step out of a circle that had been traced around him on the ground by another Devil-worshipper.

According to Ouspensky's account in his book *In Search of the Miraculous*, Gurdjieff gradually became convinced 'of the existence of a certain knowledge, of certain powers and possibilities exceeding the ordinary possibilities of Man, and of people possessing clairvoyance and other miraculous powers'. While still in his teens, he started to travel with the definite intention of finding this knowledge. Ouspensky and his other disciples were convinced that he did find it; but where he found it, Gurdjieff would never say. Even to Ouspensky, he was vague: he mentioned 'Tibetan monasteries, the

Chitral, Mount Athos; Sufi schools in Persia, in Bokhara, and eastern Turkestan; and he mentioned Dervishes of various orders, but all of them in a very indefinite way.'

According to John Bennett's account in *Gurdjieff: a Very Great Enigma*, Gurdjieff became convinced that the Caucasus, where he was born, was still the repository of some ancient secret wisdom, possibly going back 4,000 years. Accordingly, he embarked on a 20-year quest for this esoteric knowledge, during the course of which he allegedly discovered 'practical and powerful methods for Man to produce and control the fine substances' needed to produce psychic and spiritual changes in himself.

How Gurdjieff supported himself during these prolonged travels is not clear. He may have traded in oriental carpets, as he did later in life. Suggestions have also been made that he worked as a Russian spy. In any event, towards the end of his travels, he had acquired sufficient proficiency in hypnosis and auto-suggestion to be able to earn a living as 'miracle-worker' or healer.

POWERFUL CHARISMA

Eventually, Gurdjieff returned to Russia. There, he set up practical groups to work at his 'system' in St Petersburg and Moscow. It was in Moscow, in 1915, that Peter Ouspensky first met him, in a back-street cafe:

'I saw a man of an oriental type, no longer young, with a black mustache and piercing eyes, who astonished me first of all because he seemed to be disguised and completely out of keeping with the place and its atmosphere.'

He wore a black overcoat with a velvet collar, and a black bowler hat; and he spoke Russian incorrectly with a strong Caucasian accent – which was also, apparently, the way he spoke English. Ouspensky visited Gurdjieff's apartment on the Bolshaia Dmitrovka, which was furnished in Eastern style with the floors and walls covered in carpets, and the ceilings hung with silk shawls; it had a special atmosphere, and pupils who visited Gurdjieff there would often sit down and simply remain silent for hours. But chance visitors would react strangely to this atmosphere by starting to talk non-stop 'as if they were afraid of... feeling something'. Ouspensky said that another special quality of the apartment was that it 'was not possible to tell lies there'.

The prospectus of Gurdjieff's Institute, which he opened first in Tiflis in Georgia in 1919, offered as subjects for study 'gymnastics of all kinds (rhythmical, medicinal, and others); exercises for the development of will, memory, attention, hearing, thinking, emotion, instinct, and so on'. It made no mention, however, of the sacred dances or the breathing exercises that formed an essential part of Gurdjieff's system.

The memoirs of many of Gurdjieff's pupils suggest that they endured the rigorous discipline he imposed in the hope of achieving some kind of breakthrough into a state of higher consciousness that would bring with it the most extraordinary psychic powers. But it became clear to his more advanced pupils that Gurdjieff had not set up his working groups entirely out of altruism, to benefit

Disciples of Gurdjieff, left, perform one of his sacred dances. At the left of the front row is Madame Ogilvanna Lloyd Wright, wife of the renowned American architect, Frank Lloyd Wright. Learning the movements which were understood to be derived from ancient Dervish dances, below, constituted a physical discipline that was designed to give the participants a superhuman control over their faculties.

TO KNOW—TO UNDERSTAND—TO BE

The Science of the Harmonious Development of Man according to the method of G.I. GURDJIEFF.

The design, left, was for the 1923 programme of Gurdjieff's Institute for the Harmonious Development of Man, and shows the fruitful cooperation of opposing elements of life – art and music, science and technology – symbolised by an angel and a demon.

Everyone who met Gurdjieff, right, was aware of his personal magnetism and the immense vitality that he was able to impart to others. Some, however, found his appearance unprepossessing: Katherine Mansfield, for instance, described him as looking 'exactly like a carpet dealer from the Tottenham Court Road'.

Peter Ouspensky, below right, was Gurdjieff's chief Russian disciple. Ouspensky left Gurdjieff in 1924 to found a similar but distinct movement.

> **"GURDJIEFF MAINTAINED THAT THE DANCES EMBODIED ESOTERIC MEANINGS THAT WOULD BE APPARENT TO THE INITIATED... FOR THE INDIVIDUAL DANCERS, THE TASK OF MASTERING THE DIFFICULT MOVEMENTS WAS ITSELF A PHYSICAL DISCIPLINE THAT WAS TO ENABLE THEM TO ACQUIRE SUPERHUMAN CONTROL OVER THEIR FACULTIES."**

Mankind, but to satisfy his own inner needs. In the course of his 20-year search, Gurdjieff had become convinced that esoteric knowledge was not enough. He needed also to increase his knowledge of practical psychology, and for this he needed a number of subjects to study at first hand. Early in his career, his healing work with drug and alcohol addicts gave him his opportunity; and in his book *The Herald of Coming Good,* he said that he became a healer of vices both to give 'conscientious aid to sufferers' and 'for the sake of my investigations'. His work with groups of his adherents in Russia and France gave him a continuing opportunity to develop his knowledge of the human psyche. C.S. Nott relates in his book *Further Teachings of Gurdjieff,* how he met Gurdjieff in Paris at the Café de la Paix, and complained bitterly that Gurdjieff had brought himself and another disciple, Orage, so far – and then left them 'seemingly in the air'. Gurdjieff listened quietly – and then said, with a sardonic grin: 'I needed rats for my experiments.'

THE SACRED DANCE

A large part of the system was taken up with practising and performing the sacred dances that Gurdjieff was understood to have learned within the confines of a Dervish monastery. Groups of otherwise inexperienced dancers were trained by Gurdjieff in these skills, and public performances were given on several occasions in Paris, London and New York. Gurdjieff maintained that the dances embodied esoteric meanings that would be apparent to the initiated: 'In the strictly defined movements and combinations of the dancers, certain laws are visually reproduced which are intelligible to those who know them.'

What was more, for the individual dancers, the task of mastering the difficult movements was itself a physical discipline that was to enable them to acquire superhuman control over their faculties.

To the uninitiated observer, however, the dances certainly did not come over as a language expressing knowledge of a higher order. At a public demonstration in New York in 1924, William Seabrook recorded his main impression of 'the amazing, brilliant, automaton-like, inhuman, almost incredible docility and robot-like obedience of the disciples... They were like a group of perfectly trained zombies.' Seabrook went on to write, in his book *Witchcraft, its Power in the World Today,* that the main purpose of the demonstration seemed to be to show how Gurdjieff had taught his pupils 'supernormal powers of physical control, coordination, relaxation', and so on, without which – when dancing in this way – they would certainly have broken limbs.

In spite of the scoffers, who described Gurdjieff variously as the 'Greek charlatan', 'the Armenian magic master' and the 'Caucasian wonder-worker', Gurdjieff's pupils remained convinced that he was a genuine mage, in possession of occult knowledge and special powers. Orage called him 'a kind of walking god', and he seems to have had some kind of psychic energy that he was able, on occasions, to transmit directly to his pupils in order to strengthen their physical and mental states. John Bennett reports, in his autobiography, *Witness,* an incident that happened while he was resident at the Prieuré.

He woke one morning feeling ill; but nevertheless, driven by some 'superior will', he got up as usual and performed his day's programme of physical work, including Gurdjieff's strenuous dancing class in the afternoon. During the latter, Bennett felt himself growing weaker and weaker. He felt Gurdjieff's eyes upon him, willing him to continue. Suddenly, he felt 'an influx of immense power': his body seemed 'to have turned into light'.

Gurdjieff later told Bennett that what he called 'higher emotional energy' was necessary if one desired to develop oneself. Some rare people in the world, he said, are connected to what he regarded as a 'great accumulator' of this energy, and can transmit it to others. Gurdjieff implied that he himself was one of these people.

MYSTICAL STATES

Gurdjieff was also credited by many with telepathic powers. Ouspensky relates a curious experience, in 1916, when he was staying with Gurdjieff in a house in Finland. Ouspensky had been going through an intensive period of exercises that included fasting and special breathing sequences, and he claimed to have experienced mystical states – states that he was, however, unable to describe. While sitting in a small room with Gurdjieff and two other people, Ouspensky began to 'hear his thoughts'. Gurdjieff was talking to Ouspensky – but he was doing so telepathically:

'I heard his voice inside me as it were in the chest near the heart. He put a definite question to me. I looked at him; he was sitting and smiling. His question provoked in me a very strong emotion.'

Ouspensky went to bed. But the telepathic conversation continued during the night, with Ouspensky now able to send telepathic messages in return to Gurdjieff. This strange communication between them continued in this way, we are told, for several days.

Music also played an important part in Gurdjieff's system. Indeed, Gurdjieff himself wrote the music for his sacred dances, based on what he could remember of the music he had heard in the Dervish monastery. He played his own melodies on a small hand-organ, and several pupils testified to the psychic healing powers of the music. C. S. Nott recalled how he visited Gurdjieff in great distress after a severe and crippling accident to his young son. Gurdjieff led Nott into his sitting room, took up his hand-organ, 'and began to play a simple melody with strange harmonies, repeating and repeating, yet all the time with different combinations of notes'. Nott felt that Gurdjieff was conveying something to him through the music, and also through the 'telepathic means he knew so well'. A feeling of hope soon began to replace his 'dark depression'.

Gurdjieff died in Paris on 29 October 1949. His loyal and admiring pupils kept vigil over his body for several days while it lay in the chapel at the American hospital, and C.S. Nott reported that 'strong vibrations filled the place' and there seemed to be 'emanations or radiations from the corpse itself'. After Gurdjieff's death, some groups continued to follow his system in France, the United States and England. One of these was run by John Bennett at his house at Coombe Springs, outside London. Bennett claimed to have been close to Gurdjieff in the last months of his life, and recalls that Gurdjieff often referred 'to his own imminent departure from this world and to the coming of another who would complete the work he had started'. He also indicated that there was a teacher who was already preparing himself 'a long way from here', and he named that place as somewhere in the Far East.

In apparent fulfilment of this prediction, the Coombe Springs group abandoned the Gurdjieff system in 1957 and embraced a new philosophy – from Indonesia.

Prior to the interment of Gurdjieff at Fontainebleau in November 1949, below, his disciples stood vigil over his body for several days. One of them commented that 'strong vibrations filled the place', and there were apparently 'emanations or radiations from the corpse itself'.

THE PHENOMENAL PALLADINO

EUSAPIA PALLADINO WAS ONE OF THE MOST THOROUGHLY INVESTIGATED MEDIUMS OF ALL TIME. ALTHOUGH SHE WAS CAUGHT CHEATING ON OCCASIONS, MANY BELIEVED, AS A RESULT OF ATTENDING HER SEANCES, THAT SHE DID HAVE GENUINE POWERS

Anybody who sat at a seance with Eusapia Palladino could expect plenty of action: heavy furniture often moved violently as though with a will of its own; materialised hands grabbed, clasped or stroked the sitters; horns hooted, lights flashed. Palladino allegedly produced these phenomena under extremely stringent conditions and did more than any other medium to convince psychical researchers that physical manifestations in the seance room were real – even though she was at times caught cheating.

Eusapia Palladino was born into a peasant family in January 1854, near Bari in southern Italy. Her

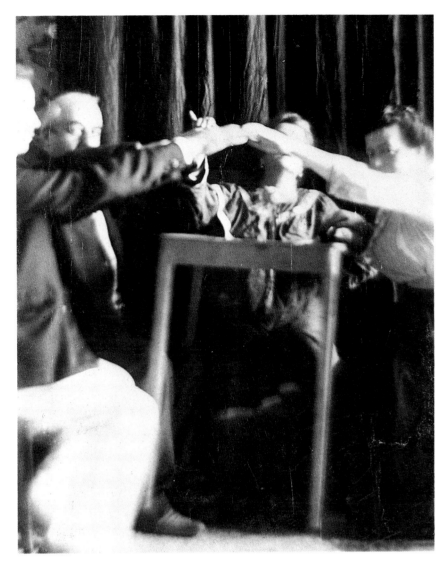

again with undulatory movements, as if they were obeying her will. She increases their height or lessens it according to her pleasure. She raps or taps upon the walls, the ceiling, and the floor, with fine rhythm and cadence.

'This woman rises in the air, no matter what bands tie her down. She seems to lie upon the empty air, as on a couch, contrary to all the laws of gravity; she plays on musical instruments – organs, bells, tambourines – as if they had been touched by her hands or moved by the breath of invisible gnomes ...

'How many legs and arms has she? We do not know. While her limbs are being held by incredulous spectators, we see other limbs coming into view, without her knowing where they come from.'

When Lombroso visited Naples two years later and accepted the invitation extended to him to sit with Eusapia Palladino, he was greatly impressed. Indeed, as a result of his experiences with the medium, Lombroso spent many years investigating the paranormal; and his books on the subject show that he finally came to believe that spirits of the dead were indeed responsible for producing mediumistic phenomena.

BOUND TO IMPRESS

In 1892, a group of researchers, known as the Milan Commission, held 17 sittings with Eusapia Palladino, and issued a report that said, in part:

'It is impossible to count the number of times that a hand appeared and was touched by one of us. Suffice it to say that doubt was no longer possible. It was indeed a living human hand which we saw and touched, while at the same time the bust and the arms of the medium remained visible, and her hands were held by those on either side of her.'

Unlike other mediums, Palladino did not sit behind a curtain during her seances. But she did use a cabinet, which she claimed helped some of the phenomena to build up, sitting always in front of it, however. Whether she and her investigators sat in total darkness, or whether there was sufficient light to see her clearly, she always allowed the witnesses to tie her or hold her securely in the chair, in order to satisfy themselves that she could not cheat.

Among the members of the Milan Commission was Charles Richet, professor of physiology at the Faculty of Medicine in Paris, who became one of her staunchest supporters. He conducted more than 100 seances with her and, as one of Europe's leading psychical researchers, was better placed than any other investigator to give a verdict on her psychic powers – a verdict that was favourable.

Professor Richet introduced various controls into his experiments with Palladino in order to prevent her cheating; and in his book, *Thirty Years of Psychical Research,* he tells of a table that was specially made for her seances.

'The legs were pointed so that it would be difficult to raise it with the foot... We thought it much too heavy (44 pounds) [20 kilograms], but we tried it the same evening. As soon as Eusapia touched this heavy table with the tips of her fingers, it tilted, swaying about, and without the legs being touched at all, it rose up completely with all four feet off the ground.'

mother died while giving birth to her, and Eusapia became an orphan at the age of 12, when her father was murdered.

Palladino was only a teenager when her mediumistic powers were revealed. This came about in a remarkable way. In 1872, the English wife of an Italian psychical researcher called Damiani attended a seance in London. A spirit who identified himself as John King 'came through' and told her that there was, in Naples, a very powerful medium who was the reincarnation of his daughter, the famous Katie King. He then gave the full address of the house where this medium could be found. Damiani went there and, astonishingly enough, found Eusapia Palladino. As a result, he became the young girl's mentor and helped her to develop her powers.

The first scientist to declare his belief in Palladino's genuineness was Dr Ercole Chiaia. He did so in 1888, by means of an open letter to Cesare Lombroso, the well-known psychiatrist and criminologist, after the latter had written an article scoffing at Spiritualism. Chiaia invited Lombroso to witness a special case – Eusapia Palladino. Part of the letter ran as follows:

'Either bound to a seat, or firmly held by the hands . . . she attracts to her the articles of furniture which surround her, lifts them up, holds them suspended in the air . . . and makes them come down

Table-turning – such as that shown above at a seance in Genoa, Italy, in 1906 – featured heavily in Palladino's production of phenomena. Sometimes, in fact, the tables became quite violent and even appeared to attack sitters.

Eusapia Palladino, in close-up, top left, is also seen left at a Society for Psychical Research investigation in 1909.

Tables feature prominently in accounts of Eusapia Palladino's mediumship. P. Foa, professor of pathological anatomy at the University of Turin, and a team of scientists, including a certain Dr Arullani, held a series of experimental seances with the medium. At one of these, Palladino advised them not to touch any levitated objects because she would not be able to restrain their movements and someone might be hurt.

Immediately, one of the tables in the room floated into the air, over Professor Foa's head, and returned to the floor where it flipped over, and then stood up on its legs again. At this point, Dr Arullani approached it; but, according to the scientists' report:

'The piece of furniture moving violently towards him, repulsed him; Dr Arullani seized the table, which was heard to crack in the struggle . . . [it] passed behind the curtain... Professor Foa saw it turn over and rest on one of its sides, whilst one of the legs came off violently, as if under the action of some force pressing upon it. At this moment, the table came violently out of the cabinet, and continued to break up under the eyes of everyone present. Dr Arullani... was invited by the medium to approach the cabinet. He had hardly reached it when he felt himself hit by pieces of wood and hands, and we all heard the noise of the blows.'

In 1895, Palladino, already much investigated, visited England to give a series of seances at Cambridge for the Society for Psychical Research (SPR). This was after two of its founding members, Frederic Myers and Sir Oliver Lodge, had attended seances with her at the home of Professor Richet and had given favourable reports.

One of the witnesses at a Cambridge seance was Dr Richard Hodgson, who suspected that Eusapia Palladino could not do anything without

The table, above, was used by the SPR for testing Palladino and designed specially to detect fraud.

cheating. Although he was supposed to be watching her movements, he deliberately relaxed his guard and Palladino did cheat. The SPR pronounced her a fraud, but European investigators were unimpressed by this 'exposure'. They were aware that the medium would use trickery if given the opportunity, and had said as much in previous reports. Their attitude was that, had the SPR controls been stringent, the phenomena would have been genuine.

MOODS OF A MEDIUM

Camille Flammarion, a leading French astronomer – and, in fact, the man who coined the term 'psychic' – was another investigator of Eusapia Palladino. During one of the series of seances he conducted, he reported that the medium became very irritable and that the phenomena became destructive:

'The sofa came forward when she looked at it, then recoiled before her breath; all the instruments were thrown pell-mell upon the table; the tambourine rose almost to the height of the ceiling; the cushions took part in the sport, overturning everything on the table; [one participant] was thrown from his chair. This chair – a heavy dining-room chair of black walnut, with stuffed seat – rose into the air, came up on the table with a great clatter, then pushed off... '

Cesar Lombroso, left, an Italian criminologist, was convinced of Palladino's powers, despite the knowledge that she would sometimes cheat.

At a seance, far right, held in Naples, Italy, in 1908, Eusapia Palladino sits between two psychic investigators – Professor Galeotti of Naples University and Everard Feilding, of the SPR. This was the fourth of 11 seances held in Italy, to investigate the authenticity of Palladino. All the SPR investigators were initially sceptical of her, but became convinced that the phenomena they witnessed were real.

ɪɪ IN THE STATE OF TRANCE, SHE FIRST BECOMES PALE . . . THEN SHE ENTERS A STATE OF ECSTASY, EXHIBITING MANY OF THOSE GESTURES THAT ARE FREQUENT IN HYSTERICAL FITS, SUCH AS YAWNINGS, SPASMODIC LAUGHTER, FREQUENT CHEWING, TOGETHER WITH CLAIRVOYANCE... **ɪɪ**

CESARE LOMBROSO,

AFTER DEATH – WHAT?

*In*Focus

EXPERIMENTS WITH EUSAPIA

In his book *After Death – What?: Researches into Hypnotic and Spiritualistic Phenomena*, 19th-century professor of forensic medicine, psychiatrist and criminologist Cesare Lombroso gives an account of the many experiments that he and a number of colleagues set up in order to test the alleged mediumistic powers of Eusapia Palladino.

At first, Lombroso regarded anything associated with Spiritualism with the utmost scepticism, even horror. However, his interest was aroused on hearing of an adolescent girl who had suddenly become blind but who seemed to have developed certain remarkable powers – such as seeing through an ear, smelling by means of the back of her foot, and prophecy – as a form of compensation.

Lombroso was utterly intrigued by such reports, and was subsequently invited to attend one of Palladino's seances in Naples – an experience that left him greatly impressed and led to many years of experimentation under controlled conditions.

Just one of the many astonishing occurrences Lombroso witnessed was the levitation of Palladino to the top of a table. As he wrote: 'It took place twice... The medium, who was sitting near one end of the table, was lifted up in her chair, while making groaning noises, and put down, still seated, on the table top, and then returned to the same position as before.' He was convinced that no one present had any part in this bizarre event.

Other curious happenings included the sounding of a trumpet which had been placed behind the medium but with which she had no contact; the sensation of being touched even when Palladino (and anyone else for that matter) was not within reach; and objects which moved from the pocket of an overcoat to the table. When the room was lit, it was found that Palladino, making noises of extreme discomfort, was now actually wearing the overcoat. Yet all the while, she had been held by those adjacent to her.

In one experiment, part of the room was left in darkness and separated by a curtain. Palladino sat by an opening, her arms, face and torso in the light. Behind the curtain, the experimenters placed a small chair, a bell and some moist clay. They then formed a circle around the table in the lighter part of the room. Soon, they saw the curtain blowing towards them. The chair of one of the witnesses was pulled at, and five blows were struck at it, said by Palladino to indicate the need for less light. Accordingly, the lantern was dimmed. One witness felt fingers touching him, and the chair that had been placed behind the curtain was suddenly thrust into his hand. Others reported 'a living human hand that we saw and touched, while at the same time the body and arms of the medium remained in sight and her hands were continuously held by those on either side of her'. There were also fingermarks in the clay.

Lombroso was eventually to write to a friend of his complete *volte-face* with regard to Spiritualism. 'I am ashamed and regretful that I fought the possibility of spiritualistic facts with so much obstinacy. I say the *facts* because I tend to reject spiritualist *theory*: but the *facts* exist; and as for *facts*, I am most assuredly their slave.'

Eusapia Palladino continued to produce convincing physical phenomena for researchers on the mainland of Europe; and so, eventually, the SPR decided to re-open the case. In 1908, they sent a team of three to Naples to attend seances with Palladino.

The members of that team were probably the most sceptical of all the SPR investigators – Everard Feilding, Hereward Carrington and W. W. Baggally. They concluded that the phenomena they witnessed, including levitation, movement of objects and the production of lights, raps and materialised shapes, were due to some kind of agency 'wholly different from mere physical dexterity on her part'. After the sixth of the 11 seances, which were held in a hotel room in Naples, Feilding wrote:

'For the first time, I have the absolute conviction that our observation is not mistaken. I realise as an appreciable fact of life that, from an empty curtain, I have seen hands and heads come forth, and that behind the empty curtain I have been seized by living fingers, the existence and position of the nails of which were perceptible. I have seen this extraordinary woman, sitting outside the curtain, held hand

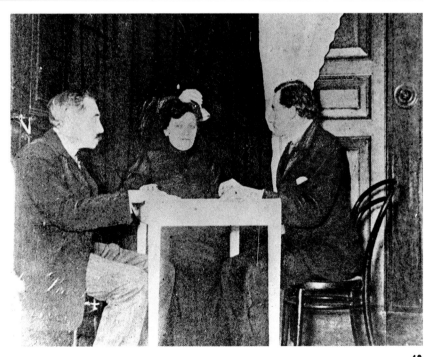

and foot, visible to myself, by my colleagues, immobile, except for the occasional straining of a limb, while some entity within the curtain has over and over again pressed my hand in a position clearly beyond her reach.'

A year later, however, Palladino was caught cheating again, this time in the United States. She had spent seven months in America from 1909 to 1910 and impressed many investigators. But at one of her seances, a man managed to slip under the curtain of the cabinet and, from that vantage point, 'saw that she had simply freed her foot from her shoe and, with an athletic backward movement of the leg, was reaching out and fishing with her toes for the guitar and the table in the cabinet'.

At another American seance, a conjurer, who concealed himself under the seance table, caught her in deceit. But another, and more famous, stage magician, Howard Thurston, testified that the table levitations he witnessed in her presence 'were not due to fraud and were not performed by the aid of her feet, knees or hands.'

WILLED BY SCEPTICS?

The man who had invited her to visit the United States to give demonstrations was Hereward Carrington, one of the three SPR investigators sent to Naples. After the unfortunate American episode described above, he observed:

'Practically every scientific committee detected her in attempted fraud, but every one of these committees emerged from their investigations quite convinced of the reality of these phenomena, except the Cambridge and American investigations which ended in exposure.'

Palladino herself never denied that she sometimes cheated. She explained that when she was in trance, she might even be willed to play tricks by the sceptics among her sitters. But her defenders argued that some of the 'exposures' may have come from a mistake on the part of the observers, rather than from conscious or subconscious cheating on Palladino's part. It was common at her seances for limb-like objects to appear extending from her body, for example, even when her hands and feet were clearly visible and being held. Perhaps, said her supporters, her detractors saw these ectoplasmic extrusions – known as *pseudopods* – and mistook them for her own feet.

Whatever the truth, there is another fascinating aspect of Eusapia Palladino's mediumship that was not challenged at all and that, it seems, would have been difficult to fake under the conditions that prevailed. At many of her seances, human-like forms or parts of bodies were seen to materialise quite spontaneously. Sometimes, they were seen clearly and sometimes they were felt through the curtain of the cabinet by the researchers.

Professor Enrico Morselli and eight other researchers had a memorable experience of this phenomenon at a seance in Genoa on 1 March 1902. Morselli examined the medium and then tied her to a camp bed in a way that would prevent her from escaping. In fairly good light, he and the others present saw six phantoms appear. Each time, as soon as the materialised figure returned to the cabinet, Morselli went to it immediately and found

The drawing, above, shows how Eusapia Palladino was caught out in fraud at a Columbia University seance in New York in 1910. Although the medium did not deny that she occasionally cheated, the Americans never gave her another chance to prove that her powers were indeed sometimes genuine.

the medium still tied up, exactly as she had been left by him.

Professor Richet also testified to the medium's powers of materialisation. 'More than 30 very sceptical scientific men were convinced, after long testing, that there proceeded from her body material forms having the appearance of life.'

At a seance held on 16 June 1901, and attended by Dr Joseph Venzano, several phantom hands materialised and stroked the sitters. Finally, they took hold of Venzano's hands:

'When my hand, guided by another hand, and lifted upwards, met the materialised form, I had immediately the impression of touching a broad forehead, on the upper part of which was a quantity of rather long, thick, and very fine hair. Then, as my hand was gradually led upwards, it came in contact with a slightly aquiline nose, and, lower still, with moustaches and a chin with a peaked beard.

'From the chin, the hand was then raised somewhat until, coming in front of the open mouth, it was gently pushed forward, and my forefinger, still directed by the guiding hand, entered the cavity of the mouth, where it was caused to rub against the margin of the upper dental arch which, towards the right extremity, was wanting in four molar teeth.'

Dr Venzano believed that he recognised in the form of the materialisation a relative who was very dear to him and who had died some years earlier. But he was not sure which teeth that relative had missing. When he checked this later, he found that they coincided exactly with the gaps that he had felt in the phantom's teeth.

Despite the fact that most of Palladino's investigators were convinced that she had genuine powers, the American exposure marked the end of the medium's international career. For the next eight years, until her death in 1918, little was heard of her. But it is known that she continued to produce physical phenomena at seances in her own country.

To this day, Eusapia Palladino remains something of an enigma, and controversy continues about her manifestations. Without doubt, however, she was of great historical importance to psychical research in the 20th century. Arguably, she was also the greatest medium of modern times.

A small, chubby figure in a bright red robe and with a halo of crinkly black hair stood before a typically huge crowd eagerly awaiting him. He turned an empty hand palm down and began moving it in circles. When he turned it over, it contained a gold necklace. The spectators were delighted. Satya Sai Baba had performed another miracle. The necklace is one of more than 10,000 objects he is said to have materialised in this way, including diamonds, gold rings, beads, books, and even food.

The miracles of Satya Sai Baba are so incredible that they automatically invite disbelief. Yet witnesses who have come forward to testify to his astonishing powers often have impeccable credentials, and include government officials, scientists, religious leaders and other respected people.

His followers run into tens of thousands around the world, though the majority are in his native India, which now has some 3,000 Sai centres to promote his teachings, as well as Sai universities. Many of his devotees even regard him as an *avatar* – a god incarnate. Colin Wilson has described him as a 'contemporary Hindu saint'. And some who have written about him find many parallels between his miracles and those of Christ.

MAN OF MANY MIRACLES

Significantly, Sai Baba's robes have no pockets and only narrow wrists: so there seems to be nowhere he could hide the 'apports' he produces.

The powers Sai Baba possesses have always been special. When he was young, right, his father even sought to have him exorcised.

When he was born on 23 November 1926, Satyanarayana Raju was a normal robust child, though he soon caused consternation by refusing to eat meat and bringing beggars home so that his mother could feed them. At school, he was fun-loving and popular. He would arrive early in order to conduct worship with other children, most of whom were attracted by his ability to dip his hand into an empty bag and bring out sweets, or everyday objects they had lost.

Despite these early signs that he was special, the Raju family had hopes that he would be well educated and go on to become a government officer. Instead, a strange incident occurred when he was 13 which proved to be a major turning point in his life.

While working with friends, he suddenly leapt in the air with a loud shriek, holding a toe of his right foot. Everyone thought he had been stung by a scorpion, but next day he showed no sign of pain or sickness... until the evening, when he suddenly fell unconscious to the ground.

When he recovered consciousness next day, he seemed to be
another person, bursting into song,
reciting poetry and quoting long passages in
Sanskrit that were far beyond his knowledge.

His worried parents consulted various doctors
who prescribed different remedies; and when these

*The Hindu holy man, Sai Baba of
Shirdi, who died in 1918, is shown
left. Satyanarayana Raju, born in
1926, 'became' Sai Baba after
suffering the physical trauma of a
scorpion sting when he was 13.
On a visit to Shirdi, he recognised
the first Sai Baba's friends,
although he had never met them
in his present life.*

seems, was fulfilled with the birth of Satya, eight
years later, though many were sceptical of his
claim. Eventually someone challenged Satya to
prove that he really was who he claimed to be.
'Bring me those jasmine flowers,' he ordered. Then
he threw them on the floor. To everyone's amaze-
ment, they landed in such a way that they spelt 'Sai
Baba'.

PHOTOGRAPHIC EVIDENCE

In time, Satya came face to face with devotees of
Sai Baba of Shirdi and he invariably recognised
them. On one occasion, he took a photograph from
someone, looked at it, and named the person it pic-
tured – though it was a man Satya had never met.
Having named the man and said he was the visi-
tor's uncle – 'your father's elder brother, and my old
devotee at Shirdi'.

For many people, however, it does not matter
whether Satya Sai Baba is a reincarnation or not.
The miracles he performs leave them in no doubt
that he is a very special person. A recurring miracle
is the materialisation of holy ash *(vibhuti)*, sometimes scooped from the air and sprinkled into the
hands of visitors, but at other times made to pour
out of an empty, upturned urn into which his hand
has been placed. This ash has a variety of uses. He
tells many of his followers to eat it, and it is reputed

failed to cure Satya, they arranged for the 'demon'
in him to be exorcised. The young boy took it all in
his stride, showing no sign of suffering despite the
ghastly treatment that was administered to him by
the exorcist.

Then, one morning, while his father was at work
at his store, Satya called the rest of the family
together. He waved his hand in front of them and
produced candy and flowers. When the neighbours
heard what had happened, they crowded in, and
Satya obliged his audience by producing candy and
flowers for them, too.

News of these 'conjuring tricks' reached his
father who was so incensed that he found a stout
stick and went to the house to chastise his way-
ward son. 'This is too much! It must stop!' he
shouted when he confronted Satya. 'What are you?
Tell me – a ghost, a god, or a madcap?'

Satya replied simply: 'I am Sai Baba.' Then,
addressing everyone present, he continued: 'I have
come to ward off your troubles; keep your houses
clean and pure'.

The reply was hardly helpful. The Raju family did
not know of anyone named Sai Baba, but others in
the village had heard of such a person – a Hindu
holy man who had performed many miracles,
including healing the sick with ash from a fire which
he had kept burning constantly at a mosque in
Shirdi. He had died in 1918, but he told his followers that he would be born again. That promise, it

*A holy medallion created by Sai
Baba is shown above. On one side
is the image of Sai Baba of Shirdi;
on the other, the AUM symbol,
signifying the word of creation.
Baba says: 'To hear that sound
one has to approach, as near as
possible, the core of one's being...
the Truth is AUM'.*

to have cured many ailments.

But it is the materialisation of solid objects
which stretches belief to its limit. Sceptics argue
that any competent stage conjuror can make
objects appear as if from nowhere; but Sai Baba's
talents – if we accept the numerous testimonies
that have been made – are in a very different
league. Often he invites people to name what they
would like. Then he plucks it out of the air, or the
'Sai stores' as he jokingly call the invisible dimen-
sion from which it suddenly appears.

Sai Baba explains that he materialises objects by *sankalpa*, a strange form of creative will power. Psychotherapist Phyllis Kristal, in her book *Sai Baba: The Ultimate Experience*, describes how Sai Baba materialised a 32-inch (81-cm) necklace made of gold and precious stones as a gift for her. She also witnessed countless other examples of his power to pick objects from 'out of thin air'.

Howard Murphet, author of *Sai Baba, Man of Miracles*, tells of an occasion when Sai Baba asked him the year of his birth and then said he would get for him an American coin minted in that year.

'He began to circle his down-turned hand in the air in front of us, making perhaps half-a-dozen small circles, saying the while "It's coming now... coming... here it is!" Then he closed his hand and held it before me, smiling as if enjoying my eager expectancy. When the coin dropped form his hand to mine, I noticed first that it was heavy and golden. On closer examination, I found, to my delight, that it was a genuine milled American ten-dollar coin, with the year of my birth stamped beneath a profile head of the Statue of Liberty.'

MATERIALISED OBJECTS

Among the many reports which Murphet collected for his book is one by Mrs Nagamani Pourniya, widow of a Government District Transport Officer, who told him of a visit she and a small group of followers paid to the sands of the Chitravati river with Sai Baba. Instead of plunging his hands into the sands to produce materialised objects – which is a method he frequently uses – the miracle man simply scraped away sand to reveal statuettes, which then slowly rose out of the sand 'as if driven up by some power beneath'.

This may be hard to believe; but Jesus Christ

Sai Baba is believed to be an avatar, god incarnate, three forms of which are shown above.

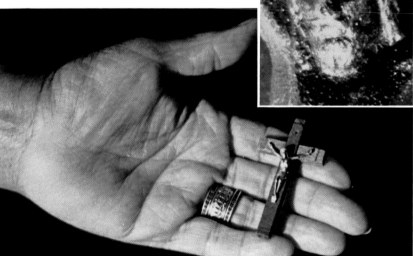

worked many similar miracles. Indeed, Christians who accept the raising of Lazarus without question should not find it difficult to believe the story of V. Radhakrishna, a 60-year-old Indian factory-owner who visited Sai Baba's Puttaparti headquarters in 1953 in the hope of finding relief from the severe gastric ulcers that were making his life a misery.

He was given a room and spent all his time in bed, waiting for a visit from Sai Baba. When that came, the holy man made no attempt to cure him. He just laughed when Radhakrishna said he would

Sai Baba often materialises crucifixes for his Christian friends. The detail, shown above, depicts Jesus at the point of death. Sai Baba reveres Christ as a Master who came to unite all men through peace, sacrificing himself in order to atone for their violence and aggression.

rather die than go on suffering, and left the room without making any promises.

Eventually, the man's condition got worse and he went into a coma. When Sai Baba learned of this, he said to the man's wife: 'Don't worry. Everything will be all right'. But when there was no improvement next day, the sick man's son-in-law sent for a male nurse who said the patient was now near death and that there was no hope of saving him. An hour later, Radhakrishna became very cold and his family heard what they took to be the 'death rattle' in his throat. Slowly, he turned blue and stiff.

When told what had happened, Sai Baba laughed: and when he visited the room to see the man for himself, he left without saying a word.

By the morning of the third day, the body was even more corpse-like: it was dark, cold and beginning to smell of decomposition. Some people advised the family to have it removed; but when Mrs Radhakrishna told Sai Baba this, he replied: 'Do not listen to them, and have no fear; I am here'.

Eventually, Sai Baba went to the room again and 'found the family distraught. He asked them to leave and remained with the body for a few minutes. Then he opened the door and called them in. To their great relief and astonishment, they found the 'dead' man conscious and smiling. Next day, he was strong enough to walk, and the gastric ulcers were found to be completely cured, never to return.

But such miracles are said to be the least important part of his work. Indeed, he refers to his psychic phenomena as 'small items'. His real mission is to attract attention to his spiritual teachings – to lead Man away from violence and hatred towards compassion and higher consciousness, and to unite many religions. He explains it this way: 'I give you what you want in order that you may want what I have come to give'. And that, he says, is to avert a nuclear holocaust.

But his incarnations as Sai Baba of Shirdi and Satya Sai Baba will not be enough to achieve that aim. He has already said he will be born again, as Prema Sai, in the 21st century, in order to complete

PROPHECIES FOR THE MILLENNIUM

ACCORDING TO CERTAIN PROPHETS, THE END OF THE WORLD AS WE KNOW IT SHOULD ALREADY HAVE TAKEN PLACE. OTHERS SAY IT IS IMMINENT

Certain fundamentalist Christians once predicted that, within the following few years, the Rapture would occur: Christ would appear, as below, and the faithful would be drawn up to him. For those who were left, years of devastating war would follow, of which the sufferings of Kampuchea, seen bottom, were to be but a mild foretaste.

Mankind has always been obsessed with predictions that the world is about to end. From sources as diverse as instinctive premonitions of utter disaster prompted by comets and eclipses, to the most complex of linguistic and mathematical interpretations of biblical prophecy and the bumps in the passages of the Great Pyramid, much time, as well as tremendous effort and emotion, have long been devoted to this single tantalizing subject.

Once, it was possible to conceive of the end only as the result of a cataclysmic natural disaster or direct divine intervention. Now, however, that we have the bomb, we can annihilate ourselves; and biblical prophecies, as well as prophecies derived from various visions of the Blessed Virgin Mary, have been adapted accordingly. In a strange way, Man, Christ and Antichrist are expected, according to some, to co-operate in some way with the bringing about of the worst and best of times.

But it is really too simple to talk about the end of the world as if, in one fell swoop, we will all be cleared away, sorted into good and bad, and disposed of accordingly to heaven or hell. During the 1980s, for instance, it was said by most of the prophetic writers on both sides of the Atlantic that for the majority of us, at least, there were seven dreadful years ahead. Let us look at what was promised by these self-styled prophets, and what was said to await us if, by chance, we survived the catastrophes they foretold, as well as what today's prophets of doom have to say on the matter.

Few of us, many have declared, will survive the final holocaust. Indeed, it has been widely suggested by certain prophets that only a proportion of humanity – but probably a minimum of 144,000 – will avoid the worst. But it is said that they will suddenly, without warning, disappear from the Earth.

This event, known most commonly as 'the Rapture' – a word originally meaning 'act of transporting', in either body or spirit – is, they say, predicted in a number of specific passages in the Bible, the most important being I Thessalonians 4:15-17.

'For this we say unto you by the word of the Lord, that we which are alive and remain unto the coming of the Lord shall not prevent them which are asleep. For the Lord himself shall descend from heaven with a shout, with the voice of the archangel, and with the trump of the archangel and with the trump of God, and the dead in Christ shall rise first. Then we which are alive and remain shall be caught up together with them in the clouds, to meet the Lord in the air: and so shall we ever be with the Lord.'

Similarly, I Corinthians 15: 50-53 was also quoted:

'Now this I say, brethren, that flesh and blood cannot inherit the kingdom of God; neither doth corruption inherit incorruption. Behold, I shew you a mystery; We shall not all sleep, but we shall all be changed, In a moment, in the twinkling of an eye, at the last trump: for the trumpet shall sound, and the dead shall be raised incorruptible, and we shall be changed. For this corruptible must put on incorruption, and this mortal must put on immortality.'

There have, of course, been countless interpretations of these words throughout history. Not all agree as to when precisely the Rapture will occur, whether before or during the so-called Tribulation; but most believe it will come beforehand. There is also debate as to whether or not babies and young children, though unconverted, will be taken, on account of their innocence. But the basic claim is simple: that members of the 'true Church', utterly committed Christians, will instantaneously be changed from their human, physical form, to a form in which they can travel through the air to join Christ, who will have travelled from heaven to establish himself somewhere in the atmosphere.

Could it be that the devastation that so many prophets foresee will be in the form of an atomic explosion, such as that above?

" THE YEAR 2000 HAS A CERTAIN MAGICAL QUALITY: PEOPLE INSTINCTIVELY EXPECT SOMETHING EXCEPTIONALLY DRAMATIC TO HAPPEN AT THAT TIME, EVEN THOUGH PROPHETS HAVE LARGELY SET ASIDE THE PREDICTION OF PRECISE DATES. **"**

THE MISSING MESSIAH

Mr Benjamin Creme was quite explicit: on 14 May 1982, he announced that the Christ, the World Teacher, had been living in Britain since 19 July 1977 and was now emerging as a spokesman for the Asian community of the Brick Lane area of East London, where he was known as an ordinary man. Apparently the World Teacher was ready now to be made known; but 'the Law governing human free will' required that humanity should look for him – he could not simply reveal himself.

When he was found, a new age would begin for all of Mankind – an age of justice and freedom, sharing and love.

Creme was confident that 21 June was the latest date for 'Declaration Day', the day on which this new leader be revealed. When journalists had combed East London and failed to find the Christ by 21 June, *Share International*, Creme's worldwide magazine, was shaken but resolute. Humanity had not tried hard enough – renewed efforts were required.

'In the very near future, it seems that certain cosmic influences will present an even more auspicious opportunity... we can, therefore, say with renewed optimism that in a short space of time *something* will happen... '

If this was the case, why was the original announcement so definite? *Share International* says: 'It does not take a great psychologist to determine what the outcome would have been had Creme given only vague dates... his message would never have attracted so much attention... '

As the year 2000 approaches, prophecy – and belief in prophecy – become more popular than ever. Benjamin Creme was only one of many voices announcing biblical fulfilment.

SIGNING ON WITH SATAN

The number of the Beast, according to The Revelation of St John, 13:18, is 666 – a number that has fascinated mystics and prophets throughout the centuries. Mary Stewart Relfe, an American author, has filled a book with examples of how these sinister digits crop up everywhere in these last days. They occur on credit cards, on the labels of shirts, on an Egyptian warship that once carried the late President Sadat (her personal candidate, before his assassination, for the Antichrist), on government forms.

She finds the number six wherever she looks: in the details of the first Apollo space flight to the Moon, for instance. 'Apollo' has six letters, each astronaut had six letters in his name, the return trip took six days, and so on. Each new sign strengthens her belief that the '666 system', a single worldwide cashless economy, is making its appearance.

She tells a story that now has a place in the canon of end times doctrine. In July and August 1980, the US Internal Revenue Service allegedly posted scores of social security cheques that carried new and extraordinary instructions: banks were not to cash the cheques unless the bearer had 'the proper identification mark' on either his right hand or his forehead. The government finally admitted, it is said, that the new instructions were issued by mistake – they were not due to come into force until 1984. A very similar story has since surfaced in Britain. However, no one can be found who has seen such a social security cheque, nor such instructions.

It is the kind of claim that makes most reports of paranormal events pale into sheer insignificance.

Commentators now try to avoid specific dates, for fear of getting them wrong. But for most, the Rapture is the event that signifies the beginning of the end. From that moment on, there seems to be a strict and relentless time scale, and an inevitable unfolding of a number of terrifying events, though opinions as to their precise order differ. In general, such prophecies agree that a leader of immense power is expected to arise following a union of 10 kingdoms – a union that some extremists have even claimed to be the European Economic Community. By the time the Rapture occurs (and imagine what a shock that will be to those left behind!), he will be well on the way to world domination.

THE LAST GENERATION?

The world, it is said, will be in an appalling condition by the time the Rapture occurs. One outrageous booklet, entitled *The Last Generation,* includes – in all seriousness – such predictions as these: capital punishment will be inflicted on those who believe that Christ died for the sins of mankind; only candles will be permitted for lighting because of a shortage of electricity; and because of pollution, water will cost about £3 a glass. *The Coming World Holocaust*, published by the Maranatha Revival Crusade, active in the Far East, picks up an astonishingly unpleasant quotation from Isaiah 9: 19-20, one not often used as a text for sermons! 'Through the wrath of the Lord of hosts is the land darkened, and the people shall be as the fuel of the fire: no man shall spare his brother. And he shall snatch on the right hand, and be hungry; and he shall eat on the left hand, and they shall not be satisfied: they shall eat every man the flesh of his own arm.'

The same booklet continues: 'Kampucheans have tasted something of the Tribulation. But even their tragedies are but a few drops in a bucket, compared with the Tribulation that is shortly to come upon the whole world.'

If the time of the Rapture seems bad, the time of the Tribulation will be much worse, so we are

Harvey Stephens, aged five, above, played the part of the Antichrist in the film The Omen. *He bore the number 666, of course – as a birthmark on his scalp. Being the son of an American ambassador, the boy was well-placed to gain the political power that is prophesied for the Beast.*

told in the Revelation of St John, an obscure biblical book. Though the list of events seldom differs between interpretations, the order of their occurrence once more does. However, two main themes become obvious. The first is appalling personal suffering from war, plague, famine and numerous other afflictions. These are divinely ordained because of Man's spiritual condition, but are often brought about by Man himself through hate and greed. The second theme is satanically-inspired political, religious, military and philosophical totalitarianism, with the Antichrist at its head.

According to Dr E.J.M. Packer, a British evangelical of some standing:

'Man is seeking to solve his economic problems in industry by amalgamations, etc, even internationally. Similarly, in an effort to answer political questions, we have the European Economic Community. It is suggested that this community will need a Supremo with almost dictatorial power in due course. In the Bible, the veil is lifted somewhat to give us a glimpse of such a man over a federation of nations. He is called the Man of Sin, the Son of Perdition and the Beast. He will be the Supremo over ten "Kings", and "Kingdoms". At first he will support the woman in purple and scarlet, representing the religious world, but later he will destroy her. In his pride he will demand that divine honours be paid to him and to his image in the temple of God and throughout the world. His collaborator will be the False Prophet... Trading will be restricted to those bearing the identification sign of the Supremo, the Beast.'

A common view is that the Antichrist, or Beast, will establish himself as potential world leader and that this will occur after the failure of a Russian attack upon Israel. This is sometimes seen as a joint Soviet-Arab attack, but is always regarded – following a prophecy in Ezekiel 39:4 – as having only one possible outcome:

'Thou shalt fall upon the mountains of Israel, thou, and all thy bands, and the people that is with thee: I will give thee unto the ravenous birds of every sort, and to the beasts of the field to be devoured.'

In other words, God will have brought about the destruction of the invaders. But, for some incomprehensible reason, God will allow the Antichrist to receive the credit. Revelation 13:4 is quoted: 'And they worshipped the Beast, saying, Who is like unto the Beast? Who is able to make war with him?' The war that establishes his power is often written of as the Third World War, but it is also frequently predicted that there will be at least two more such wars to follow.

The covenant with the Jews is seen as providing the opportunity for the prophesied rebuilding of the Temple at Jerusalem, and the destruction of the Mosque of Omar – the Dome on the Rock. (Such end times literature has no more time for Islam than it has for Roman Catholicism.) A temporary prosperity then allows the Beast further to secure his position as world leader.

MARK OF THE BEAST

And what of the mark of the Beast? Nowadays, this has come to be regarded as some form of laser-applied computer-coding, without which people all over the world – which will have become cashless – will not be able to buy or sell food, drink or anything else. This, compounded by the taking over of the Temple of Jerusalem and the killing of those who will not there worship the Beast's image, is interpreted as the last achievement of mankind's apostasy. The surviving Jews are to go into hiding, while the physical conditions of mankind deteriorate further, until the Antichrist, the Beast, decides that they must be destroyed. Then, in the Valley of Megiddo (known as Armageddon) in Israel, the final showdown takes place, between those Christians who have been converted since the Rapture and the armies of the Beast.

During a dreadful battle, Christ returns – not to the air but to the ground; utterly defeats 'the kings

American survivalists are seen, below left, with some of their supplies – food, silver and arms. The survivalists are highly diverse, but many are Christians who base their fears of imminent social collapse on biblical prophecy.

The ruins of the ancient Palestinian city of Megiddo, bottom, mark the site at which the battle of Armageddon, the last great battle between the forces of good and evil, will take place, according to the Book of Revelation.

of the Earth', and establishes the earthly millennium, a thousand-year period of peace, at the end of which all who are not already saved will be judged by the Lord.

The aspect of human suffering has been left until last, because it is clearly the most important. If any or all of these horrors afflict the world, it is not likely, surely, that it will be because God has decided that it should: that cannot be anyone's idea of a God of love. And Mankind may not be quite so stupid as to allow it to happen.

The suffering promised us by the prophets and interpreters is quite unimaginable and, not surprisingly, it is mainly derived from the Book of Revelation. The features of the divine affliction are purported to include the making bitter of a third of the Earth's water, the turning to blood of a third of the sea, the death of a third of all sea creatures and fish, the destruction of a third of our ships, five months of locusts, scorching with great heat, three-and-a-half years of drought, the death of over half the world's population, and three nuclear world wars! The picture is all gloom and despondency. Whatever happened to divine forgiveness?

In the United States, we saw during the 1980s, the Survivalist movement growing with frightening rapidity, as apparently intelligent Christians holed up in pseudo-military, all-white communities, waiting for nuclear war, the Tribulation, or the Uprising of the black population. It is not clear which they feared most; but, unlike others who dreaded the Apocalypse, they seemed to believe that weaponry would solve most of their problems.

Such beliefs appear to be a form of mass delusion, exploiting the fear and uncertainty that are natural in difficult times. But both non-believers – and probably many Christians – would insist that, merely because they are said to have been drawn from the Bible, there is no reason to consider that these prophecies must be taken literally.

> " HEAVEN AND EARTH SHALL PASS AWAY, BUT MY WORDS SHALL NOT PASS AWAY. BUT OF THAT DAY AND HOUR KNOWETH NO MAN, NO, NOT THE ANGELS OF HEAVEN, " BUT MY FATHER ONLY.
> ST. MATTHEW, 24, 35-36

DREAMS THAT COME TRUE

Jacob's dream of a ladder, as recounted in **The Bible** *and depicted by William Blake,* **above,** *is one of the most important prophetic dreams in Jewish history.*

DO DREAMS SHOW US ASPECTS OF THE REAL WORLD THAT WE CANNOT SEE IN WAKING LIFE? WHAT IS MORE, CAN THEY REALLY REVEAL THE FUTURE?

O ften our dreams take us to remote times and places: we find ourselves among people and things that are familiar, yet strangely transfigured. We do things that are impossible in waking life, or we find ourselves paralysed and unable to perform the simplest actions. Sometimes we have a sense that we possess profound knowledge that could give meaning to our whole lives – knowledge that is forgotten on waking, or seen to be nonsense. And sometimes, it seems, we are given real knowledge in dreams – a glimpse of the future as it will really happen.

The nature of dreaming has puzzled civilised mankind from earliest times, and countless strange beliefs and cults have grown up around the whole experience of dreaming. This need not surprise us when, even today, no single theory of sleep and dreaming is generally accepted.

Ancient beliefs about dreaming were usually based on the assumption that they predicted future events, and elaborate means of interpreting them were devised. Indeed, one of the oldest surviving manuscripts, an Egyptian papyrus 4,000 years old, is devoted to the complex art of dream interpretation.

A dream experienced by the Pharaoh Thutmose IV in about 1450 BC, for instance, was deemed sufficiently important to be engraved on a stone tablet that he erected in front of the Great Sphinx at Giza. It tells how, while he was still a prince, Thutmose took a midday nap and dreamed that the god Hormakhu spoke to him, saying: 'The sand in the district in which I have my existence has covered me up. Promise me that thou wilt do what I wish; then will I acknowledge that thou art my son, that thou art my helper...' When he became Pharaoh, Thutmose cleared the sand that had drifted over the Sphinx, which was sacred to Hormakhu, and his reign was long and fruitful, exactly as the god had promised in the dream.

DIVINE GUIDANCE

A dramatic story concerning a dream of Nebuchadnezzar, King of Babylon during the following century, is recounted in the *Book of Daniel*. The King awoke one morning, certain that he had had a dream, but unable to remember it. Sure that it was of divine origin, however, he called upon his wise men to tell him the dream and what it meant. They insisted that they could not tell what the dream had been, but Nebuchadnezzar imperiously threatened them with instant death if they failed to do so.

Daniel, already noted for his understanding of visions and dreams, saved the day. He prayed that God should reveal the dream to him, and that night he had a vision. He saw an image whose head was

In another Old Testament account, illustrated right, Daniel reveals King Nebuchadnezzar's forgotten dream of an image with feet of clay and interprets it as a symbolic prophecy about the kingdom. Impressed, the King is shown paying homage to Daniel.

The Sphinx and stone tablet telling of Thutmose IV's dream of the god Hormakhu, who promised him a prosperous reign if he cleared away the sand from the Sphinx, are shown above left.

Alexander the Great, above, had a punning dream, correctly interpreted as a prophecy of victory by his official dream interpreter, Aristander.

of gold, and which had breasts and arms of silver, belly and thighs of bronze, calves of iron and feet partly of iron and partly of clay. The image was destroyed by a stone, which then grew into a mountain that filled the whole Earth. The King recognised this as his dream, and Daniel interpreted it. The gold head represented the King's rule, and the other parts of the image represented the decline of the kingdom under succeeding rulers, ending in its destruction. But the kingdom that followed would be set up by God and would last for ever. As a result, the King paid homage to Daniel, and raised him to high office.

Numerous other biblical examples of dream interpretation exist. The Old Testament patriarch, Jacob, for instance, while fleeing from his murderous brother Esau (whom he had tricked out of his birthright), slept in the wilderness; and while he slept, he had a dream. A ladder reached from Earth to Heaven, and the angels of the Lord ascended and descended it, while the Lord Himself stood at the top. God told Jacob that He would give him the land upon which he lay, and promised him 'in thee and in thy seed shall all the families of the Earth be blessed'. The dream, which inspired awe and terror in Jacob, it seems, came true, for he became the ancestor of all the tribes of Israel.

Generals, as well as patriarchs, often conducted their affairs according to the supposed meanings of dreams. Alexander the Great, while besieging the Phoenician city of Tyre in 332 BC, dreamed of a satyr dancing on a shield. His dream interpreter Aristander recognised it as a clever pun: satyros, the Greek for satyr, could be taken as sa Tyros, meaning 'Tyre is yours'. Alexander took heed, continued with the campaign and captured the city.

This early example of a dream containing a pun interestingly foreshadows Freud's theory that the unconscious mind is a master jester, expressing repressed impulses in multiple puns, and creating coded dream messages that can slip past the censorship of the conscious mind.

But among speculative thinkers of the ancient world, there were voices raised in opposition to the generally accepted views of dreams. Cicero, Rome's greatest orator, argued fiercely in the first century BC that those who claimed to be able to interpret dreams did so by conjecture. And though, among Moslems, dream divination was accepted as a genuine way of gaining knowledge of the future, Mohammed forbade it in the sixth century AD because it had reached excessive proportions.

It is now, of course, highly unorthodox to regard dreams as communications with the gods or spirits. But there is a split between those academic psychologists who believe that dreams are reflections of subconscious activity, expressing our hopes and fears, and those who believe that they merely embody the 'junk' that the brain has accumulated during the day and no longer needs.

Undoubtedly some dreams – especially nightmares – are caused by complex psychological influences with roots in the past rather than in immediate surroundings. But there is yet another class of dreams – those striking ones that seem to provide a preview of future events and that probably led to ancient beliefs about divination.

SHOT IN THE DARK

One often-quoted prophetic dream concerned the assassination of the British Prime Minister, Spencer Perceval, on 11 May 1812. Eight days earlier, a person living in Cornwall dreamed that he saw a small man enter the lobby of the House of Commons, dressed in a blue coat and white waistcoat. Then he saw another man draw a pistol from under his coat, which was brown with ornate yellow metal buttons. He fired at the first man, who fell to the ground with blood issuing from a wound just below his left breast. Certain other gentlemen who were present grabbed the assassin. When the dreamer asked who had been shot, he was told it was Mr Perceval.

The dreamer was so impressed that he wanted to warn the Prime Minister, but his friends dissuaded him, saying that he would be dismissed as a fanatic. Later, during a visit to London, he saw pictures of the assassination in print-shops, drawn from accounts by eyewitnesses. He recognised many details of his dream, including the very clothes the two men had been wearing.

Although that incident is said to have been carefully studied at the time and confirmed, it does not constitute good evidence, because the dreamer is not identified. By contrast, the following dream was described by a great writer, Charles Dickens:

'I dreamed that I saw a lady in a red shawl with her back towards me... On her turning round, I found that I didn't know her and she said "I am Miss Napier".

'All the time I was dressing next morning, I thought – what a preposterous thing to have so very distinct a dream about nothing! and why Miss Napier? For I have never heard of any Miss Napier. That same Friday night, I read. After the reading, came into my retiring-room Miss Boyle and her brother, and the lady in the red shawl whom they present as "Miss Napier"!'

Such dreams, as Dickens remarks, are usually very distinct, or have a special quality of their own.

Cicero, the famous Roman orator, below, was intensely sceptical about the claims of dream-interpreters, arguing that they relied on conjecture.

The British Prime Minister, Spencer Perceval, was assassinated by John Bellingham on 11 May 1812, as depicted above. Eight days before, an unknown Cornishman dreamed of the event in extraordinary detail – even down to the type of buttons on the assassin's sleeve.

Dr Walter Franklin Prince, an American clergyman and historian who became a noted psychical researcher, said that during his life he had experienced foul dreams compared with which all his other dreams were 'as the glow-worm to the lightning flash'. The imagery in these dreams was exceptionally vivid, and the emotions they aroused, usually intense. This is his account of one of those dreams:

'I dreamed that I was looking at a train, the rear end of which was protruding from a railway tunnel. Then, suddenly, to my horror, another train dashed into it. I saw cars crumple and pile up, and out of the mass of wreckage arose the cries, sharp and agonized, of wounded persons . . . And then what appeared to be clouds of steam or smoke burst forth, and still more agonizing cries followed. At about this point, I was awakened by my wife, since I was making noises indicative of distress.'

The following morning, a railway disaster occurred in New York. When Dr Prince read the newspaper accounts, he was struck by many 'coinciding particulars': the trains had collided at the entrance of a tunnel; in addition to those killed and injured by the impact, others perished or were severely wounded when steam pipes burst and the wreckage caught fire; and the disaster occurred no more than six hours after the dream and just 75 miles (125 kilometres) away from Dr Prince's home.

John W. Dunne, a British pioneer aeronautical engineer, was intrigued by his own dreams, which often seemed to glimpse future events. Dunne proposed theories of time that endeavoured to explain dream precognition. His book, *An Experiment With Time,* published in 1927, is one of the most famous studies of the subject.

Dunne made meticulous records of his dreams. The following, which occurred in the autumn of 1913, was a typical example:

'The scene I saw was a high railway embankment. I knew in that dream – knew without questioning, as anyone acquainted with the locality would have known – that the place was just north of the Firth of Forth Bridge, in Scotland. The terrain below the embankment was open grassland, with people walking in small groups thereon. The scene came and went several times, but the last time I saw that a train going north had just fallen over the embankment. I saw several carriages lying towards the bottom of the slope, and I saw large blocks of stone rolling and sliding down.'

He tried to 'get' the date, but all he could gather was that it was the following spring. His own recollection is that he thought it was mid-April, though his sister believed he mentioned March when he told her of the dream next morning. They agreed, jokingly, to warn their friends against travelling by rail in Scotland during the next spring.

On 14 April 1914, the *Flying Scotsman* mail train jumped the parapet near Burntisland station, 15 miles (24 kilometres) north of the Forth Bridge, and fell on to the golf links, 20 feet (6 metres) below.

In recent years, several bureaux have been set up to collect premonitions from the public in an attempt to overcome the often-made objection that such reports surface only after an event. The Toronto Premonitions Bureau received the following account of a premonition, which, like so many others, came in a dream.

A Canadian woman, Mrs Zmenak, dreamed that police had telephoned her. They told her that her husband would not be home for a while because someone had been killed; then she saw a body without legs. When she woke she was sure her husband would not die, but that someone else would be killed if he went out next day. He ignored her warning. What happened next is described in the journal of the New Horizons Research Foundation, which ran the bureau:

'On the way home, his car failed electrically and came to a standstill; so he walked to a telephone to ask his wife to pick him up. A police car stopped to ask what he was doing; and as he was explaining, another car drew up on the other side of the road and the driver, who was lost, crossed over to ask his way. The police gave him directions, and as the driver went back to get into his car he walked into the path of another car and was killed instantly. His

The Archduke Ferdinand, above, was photographed just before his assassination by Serbian nationalists. The murder shattered the already fragile relations between the European powers and ushered in the carnage of the First World War.

A PORTENT OF WAR

During the night of 27 June 1914, a Balkan Bishop, Monseigneur Joseph de Lanyi, had a terrifying dream. In it, a black-edged letter lay on his study table, bearing the arms of Archduke Ferdinand (heir-presumptive to the Austro-Hungarian throne, and to whom the Bishop was tutor). When he opened the dream-letter, the Bishop saw a street scene at the head of the paper. The Archduke was seated in a motor car with his wife at his side, facing a general. Another officer sat at the side of the chauffeur. Suddenly, two men stepped forward and fired at the royal couple.

The text of the letter read: 'Your Eminence, Dear Dr Lanyi, My wife and I have been victims of a political crime at Sarajevo. We commend ourselves to your prayers. Sarajevo, 28 June 1914 4 a.m.'

The next day, the shaken Bishop received news of the assassination. And, within weeks, all Europe was at war.

legs were doubled up underneath him – they looked as if they were cut off. The police telephoned Mrs Zmenak . . . and told her that her husband would not be returning home yet because a man had been killed and her husband was needed to make a statement as a witness.'

When a prophetic dream coincides with reality to such a remarkable extent, it would seem to suggest that, in sleep, the usual barriers of time and space can be breached. And since we all sleep and dream, it would seem logical that we all have the opportunity to pass through these barriers on occasion in order to get a glimpse of the future.

John W. Dunne, below, dreamed vividly of a train falling over an embankment near the Forth Bridge. Some months later the Flying Scotsman crashed there, as shown bottom.

THE EXTRAORDINARY PHENOMENA
PRODUCED BY THE MEDIUM DANIEL
DUNGLAS HOME SEEM TO SUGGEST THAT HE MAY
HAVE BEEN A KIND OF LATTER-DAY SHAMAN

If the paranormal feats attributed to the medium Daniel Dunglas Home were genuine, then they immediately raise questions about the true potential of Man and his interaction with others. For, more than any other 19th-century medium, D.D. Home furnished the most remarkable proof of bizarre abilities – such as bodily elongation, psychokinesis and incombustibility. Impossible though they sound, these phenomena were so well-attested by impeccable witnesses that surely only the most hidebound sceptic would refuse to consider what their implications might be, both for science and for society.

One such phenomenon was touched upon by E. B. Tylor, later to become the first professor of anthropology at the University of Oxford, in his book *Primitive Culture*. He was struck by the similarities between the phenomena that Home and other mediums were producing and those that were being reported by travellers and missionaries

The bronze bust, right, is of Daniel Dunglas Home, perhaps the most gifted and controversial of all the Victorian physical mediums. Home was allegedly able to produce a wide range of paranormal phenomena, including psychokinetic effects, the ability to endure prolonged contact with fire, and the remarkable capacity to elongate parts of the body at will. It was pointed out by the 19th-century anthropologist E. B. Tylor that all these talents are frequently attributed to witch doctors and shamans – such as the North American Indian, below left.

THE GREATEST MEDIUM OF THEM ALL

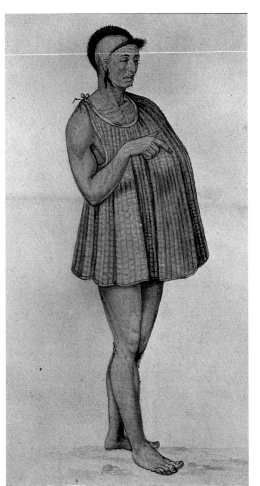

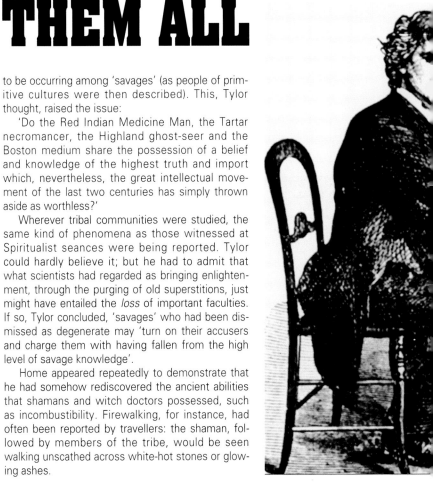

to be occurring among 'savages' (as people of primitive cultures were then described). This, Tylor thought, raised the issue:

'Do the Red Indian Medicine Man, the Tartar necromancer, the Highland ghost-seer and the Boston medium share the possession of a belief and knowledge of the highest truth and import which, nevertheless, the great intellectual movement of the last two centuries has simply thrown aside as worthless?'

Wherever tribal communities were studied, the same kind of phenomena as those witnessed at Spiritualist seances were being reported. Tylor could hardly believe it; but he had to admit that what scientists had regarded as bringing enlightenment, through the purging of old superstitions, just might have entailed the *loss* of important faculties. If so, Tylor concluded, 'savages' who had been dismissed as degenerate may 'turn on their accusers and charge them with having fallen from the high level of savage knowledge'.

Home appeared repeatedly to demonstrate that he had somehow rediscovered the ancient abilities that shamans and witch doctors possessed, such as incombustibility. Firewalking, for instance, had often been reported by travellers: the shaman, followed by members of the tribe, would be seen walking unscathed across white-hot stones or glowing ashes.

But Home's feats were even more remarkable than that. When the eminent Victorian scientist William Crookes invited him to be the subject of a series of experiments, Home began by showing how he could influence a spring balance from a distance, and then went on literally to play with fire. He first stirred the burning coals in the grate with his hand; then, taking up a red-hot piece of coal that was nearly as big as an orange, and covering it with his other hand, he blew on it until it was nearly white hot.

On a less alarming level, Home used to hold a finger in a candle flame to demonstrate that it would not scorch as long as he remained in his entranced state. Significantly, this was a trick often performed by stage hypnotists at the time. Volunteers from the audience would be called for; and those who were susceptible to hypnotism would be put into a trance and made to behave in eccentric ways for general amusement. But such shows raised some serious points, and the protection that hypnosis could give from both burns and the accompanying pain was one of them.

Later, when hypnotism became recognised by the academic world as a reality – instead of an occult superstition, traded upon by rogues – psychologists found that a degree of incombustibility could be provided, so long as a deep enough trance state was entered into by the subject. Thus it seemed that Tylor's 'savages' had indeed possessed knowledge of great importance, but which had been brushed aside by the outside world as so much 'mumbo-jumbo'.

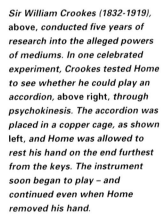

Sir William Crookes (1832-1919), above, conducted five years of research into the alleged powers of mediums. In one celebrated experiment, Crookes tested Home to see whether he could play an accordion, above right, through psychokinesis. The accordion was placed in a copper cage, as shown left, and Home was allowed to rest his hand on the end furthest from the keys. The instrument soon began to play – and continued even when Home removed his hand.

Home also demonstrated a range of phenomena that tied in with miracles frequently reported in connection with the lives of saints. As the young Lord Adare reported after a seance in 1867: 'Standing there beside me, Home grew, I should say, at least six inches [15 centimetres].' Elongations of this kind were quite often reported by witnesses at Home's seances – just as they had been commonly reported of holy men in their trance states throughout history.

ʼʼ A REMARKABLE TESTIMONY TO HOME'S ABILITY, WHETHER AS A MEDIUM, OR SIMPLY AS A CONJUROR, IS THE POSITION WHICH HE SUCCEEDED IN MAINTAINING IN SOCIETY AT THIS TIME AND INDEED THROUGHOUT HIS LATER LIFE, AND THE RESPECTFUL TREATMENT ACCORDED TO HIM BY MANY LEADING ORGANS OF THE PRESS. **ʼʼ**

FRANK PODMORE,

MODERN SPIRITUALISM

On another occasion, Adare's friends, Charles Wynne and the Master of Lindsay – Lindsay, a notable scientist, was soon to be made a fellow of the Royal Society – saw tongues of flame projecting from Home's head. 'We all then distinctly heard, as it were, a bird flying round the room, whistling and chirping,' Adare noted. 'There then came the sound of a great wind rushing through the room; we also felt the wind strongly.' In his trance, Home spoke to them in a language they did not understand, before explaining that the manifestations had been designed to show them, as it were, a repeat performance of the phenomena associated with the first Pentecost (when the Holy Spirit entered the Apostles in the form of tongues of flame).

PARANORMAL LINK

At the time of Home's greatest fame, not only had paranormal phenomena of all kinds been rejected by orthodox scientists, but the miracles of the saints had been singled out for particular derision. It was assumed they were the product of fallacious memory, coupled with superstitious awe, worked upon craftily by the clergy who would benefit if their nominee were canonised, for then their church or monastery would become a shrine.

Home's career, therefore, provided a link between the reports of phenomena witnessed by explorers and anthropologists, and the descriptions of the feats of the saints. Certain aspects of his career also accorded with the reports of the early mesmerists – some of whom had subjects who, in their trance states, developed psychic powers. Other aspects tied in with the reports of poltergeist cases, which presented many similar features – including apports (objects that materialised out of nowhere, sometimes to dematerialise again, only to reappear elsewhere).

It is worth recalling the astonishing range of phenomena that Crookes encountered in his five years of research with mediums – most of them with Home, whom he greatly admired and trusted. Crookes listed:

Movement of heavy bodies with contact, but without physical pressure.

Currents of air.

Changes of temperature [these were not subjective: they registered on a thermometer].

Percussive noises – sometimes raps, but sometimes faint scratchings, sometimes detonations.

Alteration in the weight of objects.

Movements of furniture with no contact.

Levitation of furniture with no contact.

Levitation of Home himself.

Movements of articles at a distance.

Tunes on musical instruments which nobody was playing.

Luminescences.

Materialisations – in Home's case, often of hands ['I have retained one of these hands in my own,' Crookes recalled, 'firmly resolved not to let it escape. There was no struggle or effort made to get loose, but it gradually seemed to resolve itself into vapour, and faded in that manner from my grasp.']

Direct writing – hands, visible or invisible, taking up pens to write messages.

Phantoms.

Demonstrations of intelligence that could not be attributed to the medium: the provision of information, say, about relations of sitters who were no longer alive, and whom Home had never known.

Translocations – apports.

Curiously, Crookes forgot to include incombustibility in his list, although he had been present when Home exhibited this extraordinary gift on more than one occasion.

Crookes had also witnessed some of these strange abilities in formal trial conditions. The alteration of the weight of objects, for example, had been accomplished while investigators used a gadget that made it impossible for Home to exert any physical pressure. This test and its successful outcome were also witnessed by William Huggins, a fellow of the Royal Society (who was later to become its president), and a lawyer, Serjeant Cox.

REMOTE MUSIC

Crookes designed another test specifically to find if Home could play an accordion by psychic force in circumstances that ruled out any possibility of touching it. A cage was insulated with copper wire, and the accordion put into it. Home was permitted to hold it by the end furthest from the keys; and as it was possible to see through the mesh of the cage, he could not have reached down to touch the keys without the witnesses catching him do this. Thus, if the accordion were to play, it would play paranormally.

Amazingly, the accordion did soon begin to play; and Crookes' assistant reported that its bellows were expanding and contracting, although Home's hands could be seen to be perfectly still. Crookes said: 'The sequel was still more striking, for Mr Home then removed his hand altogether from the accordion, taking it [his hand] quite out of the cage,

As depicted in a work by El Greco, left, both St Francis and St Andrew seem to demonstrate the curious phenomenon of bodily elongation often reported in legends of holy men, and of shamans and witch doctors. D. D. Home, too, was able to produce the phenomenon. As Lord Adare, below, reported in 1867: 'Standing there beside me, Home grew, I should say, at least six inches [15 centimetres]'.

The well-known stage magician John N. Maskelyne, is seen left, in action. Maskelyne toured the country with an act in which he duplicated some of the phenomena produced by D.D. Home in the seance room; but according to those who had seen both Maskelyne's act and the original phenomena, the magician's performance was no more than a travesty.

A cast of D. D. Home's hand, below, has been preserved at the Society for Psychical Research in London. Home was often able to produce materialisations of hands in seance conditions. Scientist Sir William Crookes, who held one of these hands in his own, said it seemed solid enough at first but 'gradually seemed to resolve itself into vapour and faded in that manner from my grasp.'

The famous stage magician Maskelyne toured with a 'D. D. Home act'; but according to Thomas Augustus Trollope – in those days, better known as an author than his brother Anthony – it was a travesty. Trollope had not liked Home when he had met him as a young man, but he had never doubted that his feats were genuine. Maskelyne's, he insisted, bore no resemblance to them.

But could Home have in some mysterious way hypnotised his sitters, thus providing them with the illusion of levitation and other extraordinary phenomena? This was often suggested, no doubt in desperation, by people who did not want to accept him as a genuine psychic, but who realised that the charge of conjuring could not be made to stick. In fact, there is no hard evidence that this type of group illusion is practicable.

Hard-line sceptics still maintain that what Home allegedly did was contrary to the laws of nature, and therefore impossible. However, much of what scientists once regarded as laws have since proved to be mutable: at the atomic level, they are endlessly being broken.

We do not yet know why psychic forces should operate through a medium such as Daniel Dunglas Home. But the evidence is surely far too strong for their reality – and potential significance – to allow the timidity of academics or the rancour of sceptics to block research in this area any longer.

and placed it in the hand of the person next to him. The instrument then continued to play, no person touching it, and no hand being near it.'

Crookes was not the first scientist to investigate Home. On one of his visits to Russia in the mid 19th century, Home met Julie de Gloumeline at the court of the Tsar. It was love at first sight for both, and she was soon to become his second wife. Her brother-in-law was Alexander von Boutlerow, a celebrated Russian scientist, and he took the opportunity to make what may reasonably be considered the first truly scientific trial of a medium.

One of the little games that Home used to play with sitters was to ask them to try to move a table when they had ordered it not to move: their united efforts would fail to cause it to budge – though seconds later, when they told the table it could now float, they found they were able to lift it with ease. Might this be an illusion? Boutlerow proceeded to investigate, using specially constructed scales. The table weighed in at 100 pounds (45 kilograms), but with Home's fingertips lightly touching the tabletop – in good light – the scales recorded that the table dropped to 30 pounds (14 kilograms) whenever it was instructed to be 'light', and showed a gain of up to 150 pounds (68 kilograms) when it was instructed to be 'heavy'.

In almost every respect, the evidence that Home demonstrated remarkable psychic powers is clear. Indeed, if the testimony of scores of men and women of intelligence and standing counts for anything, we must accept that he not only actually performed the feats they described, but performed them week after week, year after year. Nobody has even attempted to replicate them and show how they could have been done by sleight of hand – or, as Home did them, in good light, unfamiliar surroundings and unaided.

▟▛ DURING THE WHOLE OF MY

KNOWLEDGE OF D.D. HOME ... I

NEVER ONCE SAW THE SLIGHTEST

OCCURRENCE THAT WOULD MAKE ME

SUSPICIOUS THAT HE WAS

ATTEMPTING TO PLAY TRICKS. **▟▛**

SIR WILLIAM CROOKES

The notion that Houdini worked real magic, rather than sleight-of-hand, seemed preposterous to most of those who knew him, especially in view of his frequent and savage attacks on mediums who purported to be able to create materializations, or to move objects at a distance by their powers. But circumstantial evidence may often be very strong, and Doyle proceeded to present it in order to prove his theories about Houdini.

Doyle was not, however, disputing that Houdini was 'a very skilful conjurer'. What marked him out from his fellow conjurers was not his remarkable feats as an escapologist – extricating himself from ropes, chains and padlocks while in a sealed coffin suspended in the air or dunked in the sea, for instance – but the sheer speed with which he was able to perform them and, even more, the fact that he was able to repeat them, time and again, when the slightest slip would almost certainly have meant injury or even death. Many conjurers have since sought to explain Houdini's tricks; but although many have claimed to repeat the more dangerous feats of the legendary Houdini, not a single one has actually done so.

Some of the alleged evidence that Houdini was a medium came from mediums; some from people who knew him; and some from incidents in his life that can be explained away as chance, but may actually have been psychic.

WAS HOUDINI PSYCHIC?

TO HIS AUDIENCES, HOUDINI WAS A SUPERMAN; TO MEDIUMS, A SCOURGE; AND TO SIR ARTHUR CONAN DOYLE, A PSYCHIC WHO WENT OUT OF HIS WAY TO DENY HIS STRANGE GIFTS. WHAT WAS THE REAL NATURE OF THE HOUDINI ENIGMA?

'**W**ho was the greatest medium-baiter of modern times?' Sir Arthur Conan Doyle asked in *The Edge of the Unknown*, published not long before his death in 1930. 'Undoubtedly Houdini. Who was the greatest physical medium of all times? There are some who would be inclined to give the same answer.'

Adam, described how, 'before a trance, while Houdini was waiting at the side of stage ready for his "turn", he sat in his chair, threw his head back, closed his eyes, and appeared plunged in the profoundest meditations.' Houdini had been talking to Adam, when he suddenly broke off and sank into this state. Then, after about 10 minutes, Adams claimed, 'he continued his conversation with me as though nothing had intervened.'

Houdini himself made no secret of his skilful breath control. In 1926, a few months before his death, he took up a challenge to remain under water in a sealed container for over an hour, with no air intake – and he succeeded. His method, he told the press, was to take deep breaths before the box was closed, and then to relax, while continuing to breathe rhythmically.

His fellow conjurers simply did not believe him. One of them, Joseph Rinn, was sure that there must be a false bottom to the container, or that Houdini had somehow managed to extract air from the emergency line that was attached to it. Irritated, Houdini insisted that he had given the true explanation, and that there was no gimmick.

The first category, perhaps the weakest, largely consists of stories, such as that told by Hewart Mackenzie in his *Spirit Intercourse*. Mackenzie claimed that Houdini actually dematerialized himself during one of his performances: Houdini had been submerged under water in a locked container on stage, but reappeared, dripping, a mere minute-and-a-half later from a different part of the stage. Mackenzie elaborated:

'While the author stood near the tank during the dematerialization process, a great loss of physical energy was felt by him, such as is usually felt by sitters in materializing seances who have a good stock of vital energy, as in such phenomena, a large amount of energy is required.'

Perhaps Houdini had indeed drawn upon psychic energy, but almost certainly he did not do this in order to dematerialize: he may simply have been concentrating all his faculties on the accomplishment of his trick. And there is evidence that he was aware of this. Indeed, an English journalist, H.L.

Houdini's widow, Bess, is seen above, with the famous magician Donninger, standing by Houdini's grave shortly after his death in 1926. The great escapologist had planned – if it were possible – to free himself from the bonds of death long enough to communicate a pre-arranged code to his widow at seances held regularly on the anniversary of his death. There are conflicting reports as to the outcome of this plan.

J. Malcolm Bird, right, was secretary of the Scientific American's committee for the investigation of the medium 'Margery', who dared to take issue with Houdini over her authenticity. But, ruthless as ever, Houdini managed to 'prove' her to be a fake – using manifestly unethical means.

" AMERICAN MAGICIAN HARRY HOUDINI,

AT ONE SEANCE IN WHICH HE TRIED TO

ESTABLISH CONTACT WITH HIS

DECEASED MOTHER, WAS ASTONISHED

TO HEAR HER SPEAKING ENGLISH,

A TONGUE SHE NEVER USED. THE

MEDIUM, TRUE TO HER CALLING, WAS

UNFAZED. IN HEAVEN, SHE REPORTED,

EVERYONE SPEAKS ENGLISH. "

JAMES RANDI,

PSYCHIC INVESTIGATOR

Professor Gilbert Murray, left, engaged in many homely telepathic games that were seized upon by Houdini, who boasted of amazing success in reproducing them.

demonstration of automatic writing, Houdini offered to try his hand at it. He took up a pencil and, without conscious effort, wrote one word. 'Then he looked up at me, and I was amazed, for I saw in his eyes that look, impossible to imitate, which comes to the medium who is under the [psychic] influence.' Doyle looked at the paper: the word was 'Powell' – and Doyle's friend Ellis Powell had just died. 'Why, Houdini, Saul is among the prophets!' Doyle cried. 'You are a medium!' Houdini, disconcerted, muttered only that he knew somebody called Powell who lived in Texas.

There was also the celebrated occasion when Houdini gave what he claimed was a bogus seance for President Theodore Roosevelt on board ship. Roosevelt wrote down the question: 'Where was I last Christmas?': the answer was to be written by 'psychic' means on a slate. Houdini obtained the correct reply that the President had been in South America (a fact not generally known). At the time – as usual – Houdini declined to give an explanation, beyond insisting that it was a trick. But later, according to his biographer Harold Kellock, he did offer an explanation. He had, he said, collected information in advance – not just for the President, but for other people he knew would be on board. It was his own suggestion, Houdini asserted, that the 'seance' should be held; he had also written the answers on prepared slates, and had merely substituted them for the slates upon which the sitters thought the 'spirits' were writing.

So far, so good; but even Conan Doyle – though his detective work at seances was notoriously poor – realized that one question remained unanswered: how did Houdini know in advance that the President was going to ask that particular question, so that he would be prepared with the answer?

By themselves, Doyle's stories about Houdini's psychic powers are suggestive rather than convincing. Some simply indicate that Houdini was skilled at tricks that, though actually simple to perform, would be regarded as 'miraculous' – until, that is, the explanation was divulged. Thus, Houdini was not particularly impressed when he heard about the

Houdini also insisted that he had not been 'in a cataleptic state' – a sly reference to the 'Egyptian miracle man', Rahman Bey, who also allowed himself to be sealed up in a container, as well as lying on beds of nails and performing other feats ordinarily associated with Indian fakirs. What Houdini did not know, however, was that the deep breathing exercises he indulged in are, in fact, one of the traditional methods of inducing a trance state. They are also widely used in yoga; but because yoga, in those days, was classified as an 'occult' practice, he could not risk his reputation by admitting that he employed it.

Nevertheless, Houdini admitted that he had an 'inner voice', which, he explained to Doyle, was 'independent of his own reason for judgment', and which told him what he could and could not do, adding that 'so long as he obeyed the voice, he was assured of safety'. To Doyle, the voice was a psychic manifestation, but not to Houdini, who simply regarded its promptings as 'lucky breaks'.

RISING TO THE OCCASION

Houdini was occasionally involved in seances at which inexplicable phenomena occurred; and he did not even attempt to deny the fact, though he ordinarily claimed that there must have been some 'natural explanation'. At a table-turning seance in a Long Island country house, the home of the New York lawyer Bernard Ernst, for example, a table levitated. Ernst at first assumed that this was Houdini rising to the occasion, but he later realized, after due consideration, that Houdini could not have used trickery; and Houdini himself repudiated the charge. This was not as improbable as it may sound, in view of Houdini's detestation of Spiritualism: he did not care to be associated with it in any way. Even the great conjurer Maskelyne (who, like Houdini, rejected Spiritualism and endlessly satirized mediumship in his act) made an exception for 'table-turning' because he happened to have had first-hand experience that it was genuine.

Conan Doyle himself was given one or two intimations of Houdini's psychic powers, much to the magician's embarrassment. Following a

game that Gilbert Murray, Regius professor of Greek at Oxford University and President of the League of Nations Union, used to play together with his family and friends. Murray would go out of the room while they chose a subject, and then come back and tell them what they had chosen. His record was astonishing: over a period of years, one out of three of his guesses would be 'hits' and another third near-misses, though the subjects he was set ranged from episodes in novels to events he had never even heard of.

Houdini claimed he could do the same trick, and invited a distinguished audience – the publisher Ralph Pulitzer, financier Bernard Baruch and newspaperman Walter Lippmann, among others – to test him. While they chose a subject in one room of Houdini's New York home, Houdini was shut up in a crate in a room two floors above, and the door guarded. Yet he, too, got three out of four of the subjects more or less right. This prompted Doyle to cite it as one of many indications that 'Houdini

American magicians, as shown top, ritually break a wand over Houdini's grave in 1979 to symbolize the end of his powers. But, to many, a more fitting image is that of Houdini flirting with the unknown as he looks into the depths of a crystal ball in the company of psychic, Anna Eva Fay, above.

possessed that psychic sensibility which is the ground work of mediumship.' Not so: Houdini had instructed his brother always to repeat whatever subject was chosen, aloud – and the room was 'bugged'. He had simply listened in his upstairs confinement. But 'bugging' was new; so new, in fact, that, even five years later, it had not crossed Doyle's mind as a possible explanation for Houdini's 'hits'.

Yet some of the evidence that Houdini may have had psychic powers comes from sceptics. In *Houdini: The Untold Story*, Milbourne Christopher, himself a magician and one of the founder members of the notoriously sceptical Committee for the Scientific Investigation of Claims for the Paranormal (CSICOP), described an incident that took place during Houdini's tour of Britain in 1920, with Houdini in the unaccustomed role of the sorcerer's apprentice.

One of Houdini's first British engagements was at the Empire Theatre in Edinburgh. It was here, in the 1900s, that his old friend 'the Great Lafayette' had been burned to death, shortly after his beloved dog, which had been a gift from Houdini, had died. Hou-dini and his wife Bess went to visit

the cemetery where Lafayette and the dog were buried, taking pots of flowers to put on the grave; and by Houdini's own account, he was prompted to say 'Lafayette: give us a sign you are here!'

Apparently, Lafayette did just that. According to Christopher, the pots overturned, 'as if a spirit hand swept them to the ground'; and when Houdini set them upright, they crashed again. 'This time they fell with such force that the pots broke,' Houdini wrote; 'it was all very strange.' However, he recovered himself, attributing the phenomenon to the high wind at the time. A photograph of the Houdinis at the graveside clearly shows Bess' coat being tugged open by the wind.

Joseph Rinn, who collaborated with Houdini in his campaign against mediums in the 1920s, was also to recall in his book, *Sixty Years of Psychical Research*, that Houdini had described one occasion in his career when he was – apparently – beaten by a European locksmith, who had trapped him in a device that he was unable to open. But, just as he despaired, 'the lock, without any help from me, sprung open.'

But if Houdini had so many intimations of his psychic powers – no matter how vague – why would he so vehemently have denounced those mediums who were trying to demonstrate them?

Partly it was for the very reason that he himself advanced: he loathed the way in which bogus mediums exploited grief by purporting to provide communication from deceased loved ones. But there was, perhaps, a simpler reason. To admit to having psychic powers would have destroyed his chance of achieving his life's ambition: to become recognized as the greatest magician the world had ever known. It was an ambition that he succeeded in achieving. And although he died in 1926, Houdini's name remains a household word; he is still the greatest escapologist of them all.

THE WOUNDS OF CHRIST?

WHAT CAUSES THE PHYSICAL PHENOMENON OF STIGMATA? IS IT, AS MANY BELIEVE, THE RESULT OF MEDITATION ON CHRIST'S SUFFERINGS BY A SAINTLY PERSON? OR IS IT A CLINICAL CONDITION, PERHAPS EVEN SOME FORM OF HYSTERIA?

The curious phenomenon of stigmata – the mysterious appearance of wounds resembling, as far as one can tell, those that were suffered by Christ on the cross – is almost exclusively found among members of the Roman Catholic faith. Church records, therefore, contain all essential information for researchers in this field. Yet the Church cannot be said to be objective about the phenomenon, for it allows for the occurrence of both 'divine' and 'diabolical' stigmata, depending in theory on the saintliness or otherwise of the individual stigmatic. One criterion has been consistently applied, however: stigmatics who exploit their wounds for fame or wealth are said to be demonstrably 'diabolical'.

If such ostentatious display is indeed a factor in determining the 'divine' or 'diabolical' origin of

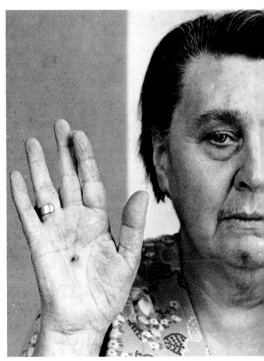

stigmata, then Elizabeth of Herkenrode should have been damned long ago. This 13th-century nun spent most of her life in almost continual trance, enacting the whole of the Passion every 24 hours, often portraying Christ and several of his tormentors by turns. Father Thurston, the Roman Catholic historian, described the scene, drawing on contemporary accounts as follows:

'Catching hold of the bosom of her own dress with her right hand, she would pull herself to the right; and then with the left hand she would drag herself in the opposite direction. At another time, stretching out her arm and raising her fist threateningly, she would strike herself a violent blow on the

Georges Marasco, far left, was stigmatised during Holy Week in 1923. Here he shows shows the wounds in his hands, and in his side, below left.

Mortado, the music hall performer, right, was billed as 'the only man with marks of crucifixion'. The origin of his stigmata is obscure, but his ostentatious display of them left Roman Catholics in no doubt: he was quite simply a puppet of the Devil.

The English stigmatic Ethel Chapman, below, who died in the late 1970s, shows the hand-wounds that occurred every Easter, as she felt nails were being driven into her palms.

jaw so that her whole body seemed to reel and totter under the impact'.

She was, apparently, dramatising scenes and actions experienced in her visions; and at appropriate moments, scourge marks – those of the 'crown of thorns' – and stigmata would open up on her body and gush blood.

SELF-INFLICTED BLOWS

Not all stigmata occur in the same way. Domenica Lazarri (who died in 1848) and the English stigmatic Teresa Higginson (whose 'blessed death' came 50 years later), for instance, beat themselves mercilessly with their own fists. Domenica's self-inflicted blows were so loud, it is said, that they were heard out on the street, and Teresa believed firmly that her beatings were administered by the Devil himself. The revered mystic and stigmatic, St Mary Magdalen de'Pazzi, was undoubtedly motivated by the ecstatic union with God that was to inspire her writings; but the relish with which she exhorted her superiors to flog her and with which she, too, whipped her novices is hardly edifying. One can sympathise with Father Thurston's perplexity concerning the phenomenon, as he wrote:

'There are many instances of stigmatisation where imposture is out of the question but in which many of the details recorded are suggestive rather of disease than of that showing forth of the divine attributes which we associate with the idea of a miracle.'

Sceptical scientists, often prefer to dismiss these stories and their frequently unimpeachable witnesses as the subjects of hoaxes, delusions or wishful thinking. There are many, meanwhile, who believe that the 'stigmatic complex' corresponds to certain psychoneurotic conditions, particularly one known as 'hysteria'. To the majority of people – including most Catholic theologians – the term conjures up an image of highly excitable neuropaths or weak-minded, pathological liars, who are given to tantrums and excessive scenes with the express purpose of getting their own way.

Call someone hysterical, and almost inevitably it is taken as an insult. The clinical meaning of the term is, however, quite different. Before the 20th century, hysteria was believed to be exclusively a woman's complaint. (The word 'hysteria' derives from the Greek for 'womb'.) But psychiatrists dealing with the effects of extreme stress on soldiers in the trenches discovered that men can suffer from 'hysterical' symptoms, too. Indeed, there is even said to be a hysterical personality type.

HYSTERICAL SYMPTOMS

Such an individual may sometimes indulge in the dramatic and exaggerated behaviour commonly associated with 'hysteria', but the symptoms can afflict anyone in circumstances of stress, heightened emotion or inner conflict. Indeed, they may actually be useful to us when we are in danger. There are even cases on record of soldiers in action who are suddenly smitten with inexplicable paralysis or blindness. Tests show that they are not malingering – the symptoms are real enough – but the cause is discovered to be hysterical. The soldier cannot face the battle any longer; but because of his training and a fear of being labelled a coward, he cannot give in to his terror and run away. Instead, his brain resolves the conflict for him, causing his body to cease functioning.

There are also cases where symptoms are revealed – under hypnosis, for example – to be literal translations of everyday sayings. 'I can't go on', for example, may be 'translated' by the brain into hysterical lameness; 'I can't face it' into blindness; and even 'it's all a pain in the neck' into the matching physical symptom. So certain allegedly holy manifestations – such as the appearance of a wedding-ring-like ridge or indentation around the appropriate finger of a nun (or 'bride of Christ') – may also be a form of hysteria.

Hysterical symptoms are, most psychiatrists agree, not incompatible with ordinary lives nor with those of the highest sanctity. So hysteria does not 'explain away' stigmata, as many Church apologists fear, but in fact could well describe the mechanism of this bizarre phenomena.

Yet most Roman Catholics still regard a 'hysterical' explanation of stigmata as an insult and a blasphemy, pointing out that stigmatics such as St Gemma Galgani, Padre Pio or St Teresa of Avila were humble, quiet and distinctly unexcitable. But a closer look at the lives of such 'quiet' stigmatics often reveals a history of mysterious maladies and an abnormal physical sensitivity. They were frequently subject to a range of inexplicable illnesses, including blackouts, fits, paralysis, blindness and so on. Many were also victims of tuberculosis, which heightens suggestibility. And, interestingly, the visions that stigmatised them also often marked the end of their many mystery illnesses.

Many stigmatics also develop the sort of behaviour associated with the shaman (or witch doctor) of more primitive societies: going into trances, having visions, exhibiting the ability to heal, levitate, prophesy, or even immunity to fire. Many also reveal multiple personalities – Teresa Higginson, Constante Mary Castreca (a 17th-century Italian nun), Mother Beatrice Mary of Jesus, and Teresa Neumann, who also spoke in tongues, for instance. It may well be that stigmatics are the Catholic Church's equivalent of shamans; but even so, multiple personality is now recognised as a hysterical symptom, and it could be that many of the 'gifts' displayed by such people, including stigmata, have the same cause.

RELIVING THE CRUCIFIXION

Teresa Neumann, a Bavarian stigmatic who was investigated by many doctors as well as researchers into the paranormal during the course of her lifetime (1898-1962), would bleed every Thursday or Friday when experiencing what has been described as 'religious ecstasy'. In 1925, she had been miraculously cured of blindness and paralysis, following the beatification of St Theresa of Lisieux; and it was soon after this that the mysterious bleeding first began.

Waking from a deep sleep, she would suddenly sit up and stretch out her hands. As she did so, her eyes half-closed, blood-stained tears would appear running down her pale cheeks, before clotting on her face. On each occasion, it seems, she would relive in her mind the entire story of the Crucifixion, and while she meditated, the stigmata would appear on her hands, feet and forehead. Sceptics have pointed out the possibility of self-inflicted wounds; but several witnesses remain convinced that these were indeed those of Christ.

Another clue to a possible hysterical foundation for stigmata comes from the component of suggestibility. The wounds of St Veronica Giuliani (who died in 1727) opened and bled at the command of her confessor, just as the Belgian stigmatic Louise Lateau and others could be recalled instantly from their highest ecstasies by the command of their superiors. The side-wound of Anne Catherine Emmerich was known to resemble the unusual Y-shaped crucifix in the church at Coesfeld in Germany where she meditated as a child. And the scourge marks of St Gemma Galgani apparently reproduced exactly those on her favourite crucifix.

This subjective element in the patterning of stigmata, and the great variety of forms it takes, also seems to argue for a hysterical foundation. Wounds have been known to range from simple red spots to cross-shaped fissures, and round, oblong or square holes in the hands; 'nail-heads' have marked the backs of hands or the palms of feet, even the soles,

and side-wounds have shown similar variations, according to how the stigmatic imagines Christ was crucified. Significantly, perhaps, there are no known examples of wounds occurring in the wrists, the site of the wounds suggested by certain researchers into the Turin Shroud. But now that this is quite common knowledge among the devout, it is thought that future stigmatics could well exhibit wrist wounds.

HOLY ANGUISH

From autumn 1911 until 1968, the most famous of 20th-century stigmatics, Padre Pio, bled regularly from his hands and feet. The wounds were exceedingly painful; his sore hands would have to be bandaged and then covered by mittens; and his shoes – now preserved as relics – had to be especially enlarged in order to make room for thick dressings.

In a letter dated 8 September 1911 to Father Benedetto, his spiritual guide, Padre Pio wrote

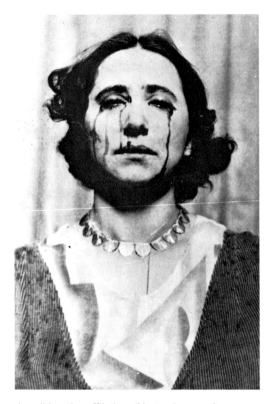

Weeping blood, right, is a rare phenomenon, closely related to true stigmata and equally mysterious.

Padre Pio, far right, experienced stigmata for well over 50 years, in the form of bleeding hands and feet, while on his chest was a wound resembling an inverted cross.

describing the affliction: 'Yesterday evening something happened to me that I can neither explain nor understand. Red marks appeared in the middle of the palms of my hands; they are about the size of a cent; and in the centre of the red part, I feel a very acute pain... At the altar, sometimes, I feel as if my whole being is on fire... my face particularly seems to be ablaze'.

But it was on 20 September 1918, shortly after celebrating the feast of St Francis (who was also a stigmatic), that Padre Pio – while alone and praying, at the chapel of the village of San Giovanni Rotondo – experienced the wounds that were to mark him for the rest of his life, and which never ceased bleeding, yet never became infected. These stigmata marked his hands, front and back, and both his feet. On his chest, meanwhile, was a wound resembling an inverted cross. Intriguingly, he bled most copiously from Thursday evenings to

*In*Focus

THE MARKS OF EASTER

Cloretta Robertson was just 12 years-old in 1974 when she first experienced the stigmata she went on to suffer every springtime as Easter approached. There were many witnesses, too; for the bleeding emanating from her forehead and dripping right down her face, started in the classroom at her Oakland, California school, in the middle of a maths lesson.

The case of this highly religious black girl is somewhat unique: for Cloretta is not in fact a Catholic, but a Baptist. The bleeding also occurs not only on her forehead but at all the traditional sites of Christ's wounds.

Several doctors have examined her. However, as the blood is wiped away, there is never any sign of an actual wound, merely discolouration. What is more, analysis has shown the blood from the stigmata to be her own. Since this time, Cloretta has also demonstrated an ability to heal. The New Light Baptist Church, meanwhile, has experienced delight at one of its members being 'chosen' in this visible and quite remarkable way.

// THE VISION OF THE PERSON FADED AND I SAW THAT MY HANDS, FEET AND SIDE HAD BEEN PIERCED AND WERE DRIPPING BLOOD. IMAGINE THE AGONY I FELT AT THAT MOMENT AND CONTINUE TO FEEL, NEARLY EVERY DAY; THE WOUND IN MY BREAST BLEEDS COPIOUSLY, ESPECIALLY FROM THURSDAY EVENING UNTIL SATURDAY ... I'M AFRAID I'LL DIE THROUGH LOSS OF BLOOD IF THE LORD DOES NOT HEAR THE CRIES OF MY POOR HEART AND STOP DOING THIS TO ME... **//**

PADRE PIO

Saturday, and was always fearful that he might die through loss of blood.

Noted, too, for his prophecies, healing gifts and facility of 'bilocation' (being in two places at once), this remarkable man was visited by many thousands of pilgrims in the course of his life. Yet the Vatican expressly forbade him to write about his stigmata or even to leave his monastery. He was even prevented from celebrating Mass in public and hearing confessions. Financial contributions from visitors, however, enabled him to build a magnificent hospital right by the monastery.

Those who knew Padre Pio well were only too

aware of the extent of his suffering. His greatest anguish, however, is said to have been caused by those who claimed his stigmata were actually self-inflicted wounds.

There have been many attempts to reproduce stigmata by hypnosis, but the only results have been a short-lived reddening of the skin, or sporadic bleeding. This pales in comparison with the dramatic piercings and copious bleedings of 'genuine' stigmata which have defied normal healing processes and stayed with the stigmatics for most of their lives. Outside the religious context, where there is no need for stigmata to take the form stylised by the crucifixion of Christ, there are many kinds of paranormal and even psychological phenomena where spontaneous formations or lesions of the skin may develop. One such case was that of Eleonore Zugun, a famous poltergeist victim, studied by Harry Price the 1920s, whose skin showed weals, bite marks and even raised lettering when she believed she was being attacked by a devil that only she could see.

In many, if not all, cases of stigmata, the effects seem somehow to stem from the subconscious mind of the stigmatic. In time, we may begin to understand the process involved. But in that case, the miraculous would become the mundane; and for the devout, such a loss could be hard to bear.

THE MAKING OF A SAINT

WHEN AN OBSCURE
CARMELITE NUN DIED AT
THE AGE OF 24 IN 1897, NO
ONE COULD HAVE FORESEEN
HER POPULARITY AS A
SAINT. HERE, WE DESCRIBE
THE LIFE OF ST THÉRÈSE OF
LISIEUX, AND THE MIRACLES
SAID TO BE ASSOCIATED
WITH HER EVEN TODAY

It was in the main street of Alençon in northern France, below, that Zelie Guerin and Louis Martin were first drawn to each other, apparently by the hand of God. They married and had a large family. All the boys died in infancy and all the girls became nuns – among them the future saint.

Sister Thérèse is seen, right, in the convent garden, holding a lily – the traditional symbol of virginal purity.

As Zelie Guerin was crossing the bridge over the river Sarthe at Alençon in northern France one blustery day in October 1858, she saw a strange man walking towards her. At that moment, according to her own account, a voice within her told her: 'This is he for whom I have prepared you.'

His name was Louis Martin, a watchmaker in the town. The couple fell into conversation – an exceptional event, for both were modest and pious to an unusual degree – and found they had a great deal in common. Both were the children of army captains who had served under Napoleon. But even more remarkably, both had at one time felt religious

Many miracles have been ascribed to St Thérèse, whose popularity shows no sign of diminishing. Votive candles offered in the hope of her direct intercession burn brightly, *above*, in the great Basilica at Lisieux, *left*, which has gradually become a place of pilgrimage.

have been spoilt. This point did, indeed, later occur to the Promoter of the Faith who was appointed by the Pope to investigate the case for Thérèse's canonisation. But he found no evidence to suggest that she was anything other than a delightful child.

Not surprisingly, given the pious environment in which she grew up, Thérèse was a devout Catholic from her earliest years. She was later to write in her autobiography, *Histoire d'une Ame*, that: 'From the age of three, I denied God nothing.'

OBSTINACY OF SPIRIT

The Promoter of the Faith did, however, find one fault in her character – a marked obstinacy of spirit – which was said to be successfully curbed except when Thérèse believed she was prompted by the will of God. It was in this way that she was to justify the dramatic breach of etiquette that she committed during an audience with the Pope in 1887.

In that year, the Bishops of Normandy sponsored a public pilgrimage to Rome – a rare event. Thérèse, by now 14 years of age, had a particular reason for wishing to join it. Her three elder sisters had already become nuns and it was her fervent desire to follow them within the next year. Not unreasonably, the ecclesiastical authorities rejected her request to become a novice on the grounds of her extreme youth. For Thérèse, however, this was merely a bureaucratic obstacle in the path to which God had called her, and she determined to seize the chance to make a direct appeal to the Pope, Leo XIII. To the alarm of the clerics in charge of the pilgrims, she made no secret at all of her intentions. The priests told her firmly to hold her tongue, an order that was strongly reinforced in the ante-chamber of the Papal audience hall. Nevertheless, when her turn eventually came to kiss the Holy Father's extended hand, she grasped it and tried to present her case. Two of the Pope's helmeted Swiss Guards at once stepped forward to remove her. But, recovering from his astonishment, the Pontiff allowed her to continue, although his answer to her request was diplomatic: 'Well, you will enter the convent if it is God's will . . .'

So, astonishingly – and against all precedent – the authorities in France relented and Thérèse was received into the Carmelite Convent in Lisieux the following year. The régime of the order was harsh even by the standards of the day. The nuns ate no meat, and from September to Easter they took only one meal a day. From rising at 4 a.m. until rest at 10 p.m., most of their time was spent in complete silence. In addition, each nun was required to scourge her naked body several times a week with what is known as a *disciplina*, a sort of cat-o'-nine tails made of knotted leather thongs.

Thérèse accepted the daily suffering humbly and thankfully for the glory of God. Discussing the use of the scourge, her younger sister Céline confessed to her that she 'stiffened involuntarily in an effort to suffer less.' Thérèse expressed surprise: 'I whip myself in order to feel pain, as I want to suffer as much as possible. When the tears come into my eyes, I endeavour always to smile.' Later, however, she came to reject the use of instruments of mortification, emphasizing instead the importance of complete obedience to God in every aspect of life.

vocations, though frustrated in achieving them. Zelie had sought admission to the Sisters of St Vincent de Paul, and had been turned down without explanation. And Louis' earnest efforts to become a monk at the Grand St Bernard Abbey had come to nothing since he was unable to gain a sufficient mastery of Latin.

Within three months, the couple were married. By their own choice, it was a marriage of perfect monastic chastity. For 10 months, they lived happily as brother and sister, until Louis' father confessor, no doubt feeling that such a state was unnatural, advised them that it was God's will that they should have children. Louis and Zelie took him at his word, and over the next 14 years they produced five girls and four boys. The boys all died in infancy, but the five girls survived to succeed where their parents had failed in entering monastic life. And the youngest of them, Thérèse, was canonised a saint of the Roman Catholic Church in 1925, a mere 28 years after her death.

Zelie died from breast cancer when Thérèse was four years old, but the little girl's childhood in the old stone-built town of Alençon was nevertheless a happy one. Her father called her *ma petite reine* ('my little queen') and would deny her nothing – to the extent that a less exceptional child might

*In*FOCUS

CLAIMS TO HOLINESS

The process leading to the canonisation of Roman Catholic saints is a lengthy and rigorous one. The bishop of the diocese in which the candidate lived first holds an enquiry and then sends the results to Rome. Here, the case is put into the hands of a committee known as the Congregation for the Causes of Saints. The Congregation now appoints two men to examine the case further – the Postulator of the Cause, who argues for the case, and the Promoter of the Faith, commonly known as the Devil's Advocate, whose task it is to search out any reasons why the candidate should not be canonised and thereby made a saint.

The life and claims to holiness of the candidate are now examined: in the case of non-martyrs, two well-attested miracles are required for the initial step of beatification, which takes place before canonisation. A five-man committee is appointed by the Congregation to examine the case in greater detail. If it is successful, it goes back to the Congregation for discussion at three consecutive meetings. The Pope himself attends a final meeting; and if, after 'prayerful consideration', he supports the cause, yet another meeting is held. The Pope can now declare the candidate blessed.

The final step in the process takes place if a further two or more well-authenticated miracles are proved to have taken place through the intercession of the person declared blessed. These are discussed at three meetings of the Congregation. A final meeting is then held, and the Pope issues a document known as a Bull of Council, in which he states that the new saint is worthy of honour.

Thérèse is seen aged 15, below, *with her widower father, just before she became the youngest nun in the Carmelite convent at Lisieux. M. Martin adored Thérèse, and her ardent sense of vocation convinced him that he should allow her to become a nun.*

A statue of the dead saint, bottom, *can be seen in the Basilica at Lisieux.*

Thérèse lies dying, right, *in 1897. The privations of her religious life took their toll, but she offered up her sufferings to God – and pledged to return from heaven to help the faithful. Her death, she said, would be only the beginning of her 'real work'.*

Thérèse's devoutness and cheerfulness were exemplary, and were remarked upon by everyone who knew her. In recognition of these qualities, she was entrusted, at the age of 23, with the care and training of novices. Then, one morning, she suffered a severe haemorrhage. The privations of her life had taken their toll. Tuberculosis was diagnosed, and she was given a year to live.

Towards the end, she remarked to one of the nuns who tended her: 'I have never given God anything but love and it is with love that I will repay. After my death, I will let fall a shower of roses. Now I am in chains like Joan of Arc in prison, but free soon, then will be the time of my conquests.'

The infirmary sister, no doubt thinking to humour her, replied: 'You will look down from heaven.' 'No,' answered Thérèse vehemently, 'I will come down.'

On her deathbed, Thérèse was brought roses. Deliberately removing the petals one by one, she touched them to a crucifix beside her bed. A few fell to the ground; and seeing this, she cried earnestly: 'Gather them carefully! One day they will give pleasure to other people. Don't lose a single one of them.'

The final death agony was a long one. For hours, Thérèse fought for breath, her hands and face turning purple, her mattress becoming soaked with sweat. To add to her pain, the doctor's prescription of morphine was denied her by an eccentric and tyrannical Mother Superior.

Many Roman Catholics believe that Thérèse's sufferings were not in vain. After her death, there occurred a remarkable series of phenomena – perhaps miracles – many of them connected with the rose petals she had plucked when she was dying. Whether or not the rose is responsible, as some people think, these events defy rational explanation.

Take the case of Ferdinand Aubry. A man of 60, he was admitted in 1910 to the hospital of the Little Sisters of the Poor in Lisieux for treatment of ulcers of the tongue. His condition deteriorated rapidly,

and gangrene set in, causing the tongue to split and then fall apart. Medical opinion gave the man only a few days to live. In desperation, the Sisters begged one of Thérèse's rose petals from the nearby Carmelite convent, and Ferdinand was induced to swallow it. The following day, he was cured. His tongue, however, was so badly damaged that it took the nuns some minutes to interpret his first attempts at speech to mean: 'When will my tongue come back?' Sadly, they shook their heads. But three weeks later, as contemporary photographs attest, Ferdinand's tongue was restored. It was now whole and entire.

A year earlier, a Scotswoman, Mrs Dorans, had been admitted to a Glasgow hospital with an abdominal tumour. Having taken no food for 10 weeks, she was failing fast and her doctor gave her just days to live. Prayers were offered to Thérèse for her recovery by the local Catholic community.

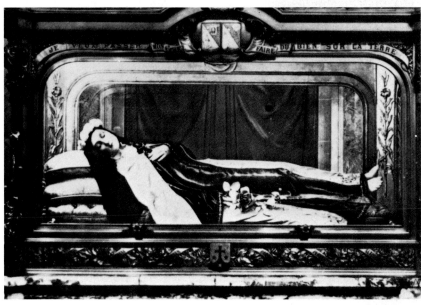

On the night when doctors expected her to die, Mrs Dorans felt what she later described as 'a light touch on her shoulder', although there was no one in the room apart from her sleeping daughter. Mrs Dorans then fell asleep and woke at 5.30 a.m., demanding tea and rolls. Later, doctors who examined her discovered that the tumour had regressed spontaneously, leaving a harmless lump the size of a marble.

A gardener's wife, Madame Jouanne, was rushed to a Paris hospital with peritonitis in 1912. She was operated on immediately, but so much pus was found when her stomach was opened that she was immediately sewn up and simply left to die. But the priest who came to give her the last rites slipped a little silk purse containing one of the miraculous rose petals under her pillow. It seemed to succeed where medicine had failed, for Madame Jouanne made an instant recovery. She left hospital a week later and lived for many years afterwards.

WORLDWIDE CONSPIRACY?

Comparable stories of the intercession of Thérèse have subsequently been gathered from Austria, Belgium, Spain, Switzerland, Italy, Africa, the United States, Canada and China. The authenticity of many of the cases is unquestionable – unless, as one writer put it, one is 'prepared to believe in a worldwide conspiracy of priests, nuns, doctors and men and women of every rank and condition'.

A mere 20 years after her death, the Church acceded to the tumultuous clamour that Thérèse be officially venerated as a saint, and the process of investigating her case began. Contrary to popular opinion, this process is, in modern times, a rigorous one. At least four miraculous cases must be proved to the satisfaction of a panel of medical specialists. We have space to put forward just two of the cases. Sister Louise de St Germain was considered to be dying of a stomach ulcer. On the night of 10 September 1915, she dreamt that Thérèse appeared to her and promised her recovery. When she woke next morning, her bed was surrounded by rose petals: no one could explain how they got there. Her condition, however, grew worse until the

morning of 25 September, when she awoke to find herself completely recovered. Her cure is certified by a series of X-ray photographs.

Charles Anne was studying for the priesthood when, in 1906, he contracted tuberculosis. It had spread to both lungs, and he had suffered a number of severe haemorrhages. As the case was pronounced beyond the scope of earthly medicine, he was persuaded to wear around his neck a silk purse containing some of the saint's hair. He tells of his forthright prayer to Thérèse: 'I did not come to this seminary to die: I came to serve God. You must cure me.'

The next morning, his prayer was answered and he was cured from that day on. The doctor who was in attendance affirmed the cure to be 'absolutely extraordinary and inexplicable from a scientific point of view'.

What distinguishes the miracles associated with Thérèse from those of many other saints of the Roman Catholic Church is that they occurred in our time and have been submitted to scientific scrutiny. Indeed, Pope Pius XI and his cardinals needed little time to assess the evidence presented to them by their expert panel. In each of the cases examined, the evidence that was cited was incontrovertible. As we find in the Apostolic Decree proclaiming the sanctity of Thérèse of Lisieux: 'Each instance involved the healing of an organic malady, one produced by pathological and anatomical lesion rigorously determined... such that the forces of nature... could not heal.'

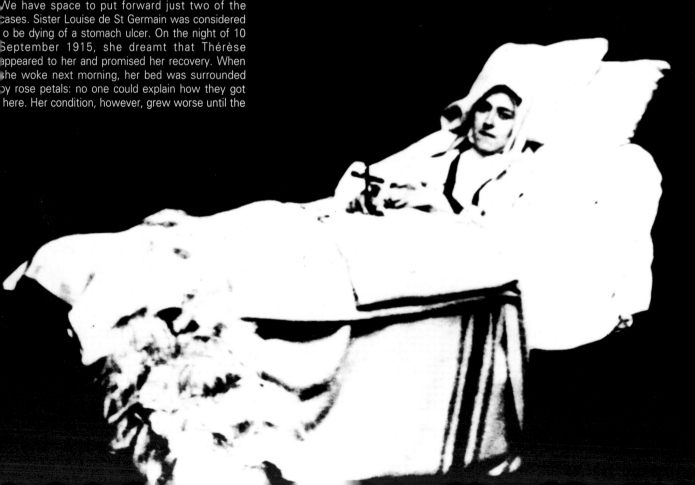

YOUNG VISIONARIES OF OUR LADY

THE VIRGIN MARY, IT IS CLAIMED, HAS APPEARED MANY TIMES IN THE 20TH CENTURY, MOSTLY TO CHILDREN – AND FREQUENTLY BEARING WARNINGS OF APOCALYPTIC DISASTERS

The visionary events at La Salette and Lourdes in France, at Knock in Ireland and at Llanthony in Wales, all happened in the 19th century. The first three sites have become major centres of pilgrimage, but Llanthony is nearly forgotten – perhaps because of inaccessibility, or because there is no Catholic tradition in Wales. In three of the reports, it was claimed that healing accompanied the visions. Three of the cases also prominently featured children. Two of the figures spoke and prophesied: two did not. But there are marked similarities among the descriptions of the figures in all these cases. And, in all of them, the experience is reported as having had a lasting effect on the witnesses .

The 20th century has seen no abatement in the frequency of visions, nor in their complexity:

One of the most famous modern visions was that at Fatima, Portugal, in 1917, in which three children, Jacinta, Francisco and Lucia, right, saw and spoke with 'the Lady of the Rosary'. Thousands of people witnessed extraordinary phenomena, while the children apparently spoke to 'the Lady' every month for six months. Fatima, below, is now a centre of pilgrimage.

JACINTA   FRANCISCO   LUCIA

modern photographic and recording techniques have, in fact, enabled details to reach an eager audience of believers. A second group of cases is even more widespread – and, again, there are many features that resemble those in earlier reports. The visionary figure speaks; and, frequently, there is extensive prophecy. The figure seen is apparently much the same in all the cases, and subsequent healings are widely claimed. What is more, in the three major cases that follow, the original and prominent witnesses are again children.

The apparently miraculous events at Fatima, Portugal, in 1917, are well-known, particularly for the 'Dance of the Sun' that ended the last vision in the series of six, and for the mystery surrounding the prophecies said to have been given by the Virgin to the young witnesses – Lucia dos Santos, aged nine, Francisco Marto, aged eight, and his sister Jacinta, aged six. They were looking after sheep just outside Fatima when they saw the apparition of a boy, aged about 15, who exhorted them to pray. The 'angel', as they called him, appeared to them twice more that year, but it is the series of events that began on 13 May 1917 that has since made Fatima world-famous.

FROM OUT OF A CLEAR SKY

The three children were once again out tending their families' flocks when a sudden flash of lightning – in a clear sky – sent them scurrying for shelter. But no rain came; instead, they saw an apparition of a beautiful young woman, aged about 18. Lucia talked to her while Jacinta looked on. The vision said she had come from heaven and that she would reappear on the 13th of every month, for a period of six months.

The children agreed that they would keep the story of the vision to themselves, but when they got home, Jacinta blurted it out. The news, predictably, spread like wildfire, and soon crowds gathered outside Fatima on the 13th of every month.

The vision was seen – although only by the three children – every month from May to September, while the attendant crowds grew. On 13 October, some 70,000 people were present when the phenomenon that came to be known as the 'Dance of the Sun' took place – although by no means everyone saw it. It has been described thus in a Catholic pamphlet:

'The rain stopped suddenly, and through a rift, or hole, in the clouds, the sun was seen like a silvery disc. It then seemed to rotate, paused, and rotated a second or third time, emitting rays of various

Pilgrims are seen arriving at the shrine at Beauraing, Belgium, above. It was built in the 1930s after five children, shown right, from two poor families, claimed to have seen and spoken with the Virgin over 30 times. Despite the number of alleged communications, the 'Lady' said little of any consequence. But even so, the story of the visions seems to have answered a deep need among Catholics, who still flock regularly to the shrine in great numbers.

colours. Then it seemed to approach the earth, radiating a red light, and an intense heat. The crowd fell into a panic, thinking the world was ending, and then into tumultuous devotion.'

It is unfortunate that the only photographs said to exist of this event appear to be fakes: certainly, they are less than convincing.

The figure itself was described as: 'A beautiful Lady, who seemed to be less than 18 years old. She wore a white robe, and her head was covered with a white veil. Her hands, clasped in prayer, held a rosary.'

The matter of the prophecies is most intriguing. The first two, supposedly given to Lucia in 1917, are less convincing for being revealed after their alleged fulfilment, in 1936 and 1941; but the third prophecy of Fatima remains one of the great mysteries. Said to have been given to Lucia on 13 July 1917, it was passed in secrecy to the Vatican, and is said to have been opened in secrecy by the Pope in either 1942 or 1960. Contrary to Lucia's apparent instructions, no official information has been given as to what it contains, but journalists and religious extremists have made a variety of guesses.

// THE FIGURE ITSELF WAS DESCRIBED

AS A BEAUTIFUL LADY, WHO SEEMED

TO BE LESS THAN 18 YEARS OLD.

SHE WORE A WHITE ROBE, AND HER

HEAD WAS COVERED WITH A WHITE

VEIL. HER HANDS, CLASPED IN

PRAYER, HELD A ROSARY. //

have demonstrated genuineness. Lengthy, learned and unconvinced accounts of the events were recorded by the Catholic historians, Herbert Thurston and Jean Helle. The visions were also used as propaganda in battles in national and Church politics.

Thurston and Helle's description of the Lady is quite standard. It runs as follows:

'They saw her shining form as she stood on what appeared to be a small cloud. Her white dress seemed to be touched with reflections of blue light, and her hair was covered by a white mantle. From her head came short rays of light, which gave the appearance of a crown. Her hands were joined, and she was looking towards heaven.'

One of the children claimed that the vision revealed her golden heart to her; but despite a continued stress on the significance of the Immaculate Conception, there was little meaning in what the figure had to say. Nonetheless, the huge crowds were prepared to accept the children's word about

Purportedly, it refers to appalling, worldwide war in the latter half of this century, to division within the Church, to the rise of Satan, and to the only gradual victory of Christ. There is a rumour that, in 1977, Christ himself appeared to an anonymous Catholic to state that the secret 'must be known by all by now', and clearly there is a widespread feeling that the facts – if facts there be – are being wilfully withheld.

THE BLESSED VIRGIN

The visions at Beauraing, Belgium, which lasted from November 1932 to January 1933, introduced a number of new elements to the subject of Marian visions. They were witnessed by, and only by, five children from two poor families, aged from 9 to 15. Thirty-three visions were said to have been seen and, although there was no independent verification, some of the visions were attended by very large crowds indeed. One fairly objective account tells of the first vision:

'On 29 November 1932, four children at Beauraing went to meet a friend from her convent school. After praying . . . in the garden of the convent, one of them rang the doorbell. They all waited, expecting one of the sisters to open the door. Suddenly, as Andrée was looking towards the viaduct, she cried out: "I see the light." "It must be the headlight of a car," answered one of the other children. All looked in the direction of the source of the light. "Something is moving there – is it a man or what?" they asked each other. Then Albert Voisin shouted: "This is the Blessed Virgin". All looked again, and all were convinced that it was the Blessed Virgin walking on the bridge... This was the beginning of the 33 apparitions... at one time, 30,000 people crowded around the site during the apparition, though only the children were favoured.'

One of the new elements at Beauraing was the depth of investigation relating to the claimed visions – including tests of the children's trance state, using lighted matches and a penknife, that seem to

In the Spanish village of Garabandal, that lies in the valley, top, four young children, above, began to see visions of angels – which, they were told, were to herald the vision of the Virgin herself. She is said to have appeared an astonishing 2,000 times over a four-year period. Sometimes, she was accompanied by angels and once by what the children described as 'the eye of God'. During their visions, they became entranced, parading about in 'ecstatic marches' or falling backwards in perfect synchronisation. Yet one of the children, Maria Cruz Gonzales, has since confessed that some of her 'trances' were fakes.

the vision, planted firmly as it was in the tradition of Lourdes. Though independent commentators had serious doubts, and there was little objective evidence, believers continued to flock to Beauraing.

A series of visions more plausible to both the serious researcher and the Church commenced at Garabandal, a small village in north-west Spain, on 18 June 1961. Again, four young children, all girls aged 11 and 12, were the only witnesses to the Lady herself. She spoke at length and in detail, with prophecy and admonition. Astonishingly, the figure is said to have appeared to the children some 2,000

 BEFORE THE CHILDREN . . .

THE VIRGIN APPEARED WITH

TWO ANGELS, ONE ON EACH SIDE.

ABOVE THE VIRGIN WAS A LARGE

EYE THAT SEEMED TO THE CHILDREN

TO BE THE EYE OF GOD.

times in four years. Considerable evidence exists of related healings – including one restoration of sight – and the village has since become a major centre of pilgrimage.

The events commenced with nine appearances of an angel, warning the children that the Virgin would appear to them as 'Our Lady of Carmel'. Thus, even for the Virgin's first appearance, there were many witnesses present. 'Before the children . . . the Virgin appeared with two angels, one on each side. Above the Virgin was a large eye that seemed to the children to be the eye of God.' They later described her in these terms:

'She has a white dress, a blue cape, a crown of golden stars. She holds between her fine slender hands a brown scapular [cloak] except when she carries the Child in her arms. She has long chestnut hair with a parting in the middle. Her face is oval with a very delicate nose, a very pretty mouth with well-traced lips. She appears to be 18, and is on the tall side.'

The children, from their photographs, look cheerful and sensible enough. Yet while they saw the visions and spoke with the Lady, countless numbers of pilgrims and others watched them, and the doctors and investigators got on with their duties. The children seem to have been in genuine trances, and were oblivious to intrusions into their communication. Interestingly, they were apt to fall backwards (as do many subjects of conversion, faith healing and exorcism), sometimes together as if synchronised, or to link arms and parade backwards and forwards in 'ecstatic marches'.

The messages they received were similar to those given at Fatima. They consist mainly of warnings and expressions of concern. A sequence of events is outlined: that there will first be a warning, of which everyone on Earth will be aware, then a miracle will occur at the Spanish village of Garabandal – of which Conchita, one of the witnesses, now living in the USA, will give eight days' warning. As a result of this miracle, the USSR (as it then was) will be converted wholesale to Christianity, and a 'permanent supernatural sign will remain until the end of time'. If the world does not then repent, the chastisement will follow.

Veronica Leuken, the 'Bayside seeress' from New York, claimed she had visions of the Virgin, who blessed her Polaroid camera so that it would take pictures with strange effects, as shown bottom, *especially the appearance of the so-called 'Ball of Redemption',* below. *Critics, however, think it resembles a thumb over the lens. Veronica claims the Virgin imparts warnings concerned with the laxity of morals in the modern world and the threat of 'satanic' influence on the Church. But none of these prophecies seems to concern specific events.*

Unfortunately, one of the children, Maria Cruz Gonzales, has since told interviewers that some of their 'ecstasies' were certainly faked, adding that they used them as a ruse to get away from the town to play. The others, however, have always maintained that their visions and trances were indeed genuine.

UNIVERSAL SIGHTINGS

Children the world over attest to having seen Our Lady. In 1933, again in Belgium, eleven-year-old Mariette Beco saw the Virgin of the Poor on a white cloud some five feet [1.5 metres] away. More recently, too, in 1987, at Hrushiv in the Ukraine, a girl of eleven, Marina Kizyu, saw the Virgin Mary dressed in red and blue in a deserted church, dating from the 16th century, where a previous vision had occurred, and where many have since been witness to Our Lady, seen both weeping and in prayer.

The consistent, and yet inconstant, appearance of the Virgin herself – changing in age, perhaps according to the age of the witness, and changing in title and characteristics, seemingly according to the need and the situation – gives an impression that the visions may only be different versions of a similar psychological archetype, and that there may be no objective reality to all or any of the figures. But against this, we have to balance the fact that most of the visions have been seen by unsophisticated children, apparently unprompted. Can we really expect them to come up with such consistent stories? There is also the matter of the many healings and prophecies. Would a psychological illusion have such effects?

There are, of course, no simple answers. But the evidence of thousands of witnesses points to the fact that something unusual has indeed occurred at such places as Fatima and Lourdes. Certainly, until we have a great deal more evidence, we are in no position either to decry or dismiss any sincerely held belief based on these undoubtedly inspiring experiences.

THE SINKING OF THE TITANIC, THE ASSASSINATIONS OF THE KENNEDY BROTHERS, AND THE ABERFAN DISASTER – ALL HAVE BEEN THE SUBJECT OF REMARKABLE SUCCESSES ON THE PART OF THOSE WITH THE EXTRAORDINARY GIFT OF PRECOGNITION

THE WARNING VOICE

A t 5 o'clock one morning in 1979, a knock at her apartment door woke Helen Tillotson from a very deep sleep. Suddenly, she heard her mother calling out: 'Helen, are you there? Let me in!' Helen hurried to the door to find out what was wrong. Her mother, Mrs Marjorie Tillotson, who lived in a Philadelphia apartment block just across the street, demanded to know why Helen had been knocking on her door a few minutes earlier.

Helen, 26, assured her mother that she had gone to bed at 11 o'clock the previous night and had not woken at all until she heard her mother knocking at the door. 'But I saw you. I spoke to you,' said Mrs Tillotson. She said Helen had told her to follow her home immediately without asking questions.

Suddenly, there was a loud noise from outside. Both women rushed to the window: across the street, a gas leak in Mrs Tillotson's block had caused an explosion, and her apartment was gutted. 'If she had been asleep there at the time,' said a fire chief, 'I doubt whether she would have got out alive.'

Had Helen been sleep-walking? Or did her mother have a psychic vision? Whatever the explanation, either mother or daughter had apparently sensed the danger of an explosion, and saved Mrs Tillotson's life. Such incidents are known as premonitions; and although they are rare, enough cases have been documented to suggest that some people are able to catch a glimpse of the future.

PREMONITION OF DEATH

Early in 1979, Spanish hotel executive Jaime Castell had a dream in which a voice told him he would never see his unborn child, which was due in three months. Convinced that he would die, Castell took out a £50,000 insurance policy – payable only on his death, with no benefits if he lived. Weeks later, as he drove from work at a steady 50 mph (80 km/h), another car travelling in the opposite direction at over 100 mph (160 km/h) went out of control, hit a safety barrier, somersaulted and landed on top of Castell's car. Both drivers were killed instantly.

After paying the £50,000 to Castell's widow, a spokesman for the insurance company said that a death occurring so soon after such a specific policy had been taken out would normally have to be investigated thoroughly. 'But this incredible accident rules out any suspicion. A fraction of a second either way and he would have escaped.'

Sometimes a number of people will even have forebodings of the same event. Many of them have no direct connection with the tragedy they foresee; but some, like Eryl Mai Jones, become its victims. On 20 October 1966, this nine-year-old Welsh girl told her mother she had dreamt that, when she had gone to school, it was not there. 'Something black had come down all over it,' she said. Next day she went to school in Aberfan – and half a million tons of coal waste slithered down onto the mining village, killing Eryl and 139 others, most of them children.

After the disaster, many people claimed to have had premonitions about it. They were investigated

The terrible events of 21 October 1966, when a large part of the Welsh mining village of Aberfan, above, was obliterated by coal waste, were foreseen by many people. Among them was nine-year-old Eryl Mai Jones (inset), who became one of the victims.

The Titanic, the 'safest ocean liner ever built,' sank on her maiden voyage in 1912. Journalist W.T. Stead, shown far right, one of the many who drowned, had published a strangely prophetic story a few years earlier about a similar tragedy.

46

by a London psychiatrist, Dr John Barker, who narrowed them down to 60 he felt were genuine. So impressed was he by this evidence for premonitions of the tragedy that he helped set up the British Premonitions Bureau, to record and monitor such occurrences. It was hoped the Bureau could be used to give early warning of similar disasters and enable lives to be saved.

When Dr Barker analysed the Aberfan premonitions, he noticed that there had been a gradual build-up during the week before the Welsh tip buried the school, reaching a peak on the night before the tragedy. Two Californian premonitions bureaux – one at Monterey, south of San Francisco, the other at Berkeley – have since sifted through predictions from members of the public in the hope of detecting a similar pattern.

Sceptics often point out that information about premonitions is published only after the event, and that the vast majority of such predictions are discarded when they are found to be wrong. This may be true in many cases, but there are exceptions.

PROPHET ARRESTED

A Scottish newspaper, the *Dundee Courier & Advertiser,* carried a story on 6 December 1978, headlined 'Prophet didn't have a ticket'. It told of the appearance of Edward Pearson, 43, at Perth Sheriff Court, charged with travelling on the train from Inverness to Perth on 4 December without paying the proper fare.

Pearson – described as 'an unemployed Welsh prophet' – was said to have been on his way to see the Minister of the Environment to warn him about an earthquake that would hit Glasgow in the near future. The *Courier*'s readers doubtless found it very amusing. But they were not so amused by the earthquake that shook them in their beds three weeks later, causing damage to buildings in Glasgow and other parts of Scotland. Earthquakes in Britain are rare; and prophets who predict them are even rarer.

But the most remarkable prophecy ever made must surely be the story of the *Titanic,* the great ocean liner which sank on her maiden voyage in 1912 with terrible loss of life. In 1898, a novel by a struggling writer, Morgan Robertson, had predicted the disaster with uncanny accuracy.

Robertson's story told of a 70,000-tonne vessel, the safest ocean liner in the world, which hit an iceberg in the Atlantic on her maiden voyage. She sank and most of her 2,500 passengers were lost because, incredibly, the liner had only 24 lifeboats – less than half the number needed to save all the passengers and crew on board.

FICTION BECOMES FACT

On 14 April 1912, the real-life tragedy occurred as the 66,000-tonne *Titanic* was making her maiden voyage across the Atlantic. She, too, hit an iceberg; she, too, sank. And, like the liner in the novel, she did not have enough lifeboats on board – only 20, in fact – and there was terrible loss of life. Of the 2,224 people on board the luxury liner, 1,513 perished in the icy waters. Robertson even came remarkably close to getting the vessel's name right – he had called it the *SS Titan.*

Curiously, another work of fiction about a similar tragedy had appeared in a London newspaper some years earlier. The editor was a distinguished journalist, W.T. Stead, who added a prophetic note to the end of the story: 'This is exactly what might take place, and what will take place, if liners are sent to sea short of boats.' By a particularly ironic twist of fate, Stead was one of the passengers on the *Titanic* who died for that very reason.

Such cases are rare, however, and for every prediction that is fulfilled there are perhaps a thousand that are not. In 1979, the Mind Science Foundation of San Antonio, Texas, USA, came up with a novel experiment to test how accurately people could predict an event. The American Skylab space station had begun to fall out of orbit and, although it was known for certain that it

would eventually fall to Earth, scientists did not know when this would occur nor where it would land. The foundation therefore invited people known to have psychic powers – and anyone else who wanted to participate – to predict the date of Skylab's fall and the spot on Earth where its remains would land. It called the exercise 'Project Chicken Little', and over 200 people responded to the appeal. Their predictions were analysed and published before Skylab fell. Virtually all were wrong: very few even came close to the date of Skylab's return (11 June), and even fewer guessed that it would land in Australia.

BOMBS AND ASSASSINATIONS

While such experiments to prove that the future can be predicted have not been very successful, some individuals nevertheless seem to excel at prophecy. Nostradamus, for example, the 16th-century seer, made many prophecies that have apparently come true. Not everyone agrees with their interpretation, however. Take this one for example:

'Near the harbour and in two cities will be two scourges, the like of which have never been seen. Hunger, plague within, people thrown out by the sword will cry for help from the great immortal God.'

But what does it predict? Nostradamus' followers say it is a prediction of the atom bomb attacks on Nagasaki and Hiroshima in 1945. But no one could have used his prophecy to foretell these events. In other words, it is hindsight that gives credibility to writing such as this.

Jeane Dixon, a modern seer, successfully predicted the assassinations of President John F. Kennedy, his brother, Robert Kennedy, and civil rights leader Martin Luther King. Intriguingly, her premonition of the American President's murder came 11 years before the event and before he had even been elected President.

A devout woman, she had gone to St Matthew's Cathedral in Washington one morning in 1952 to pray, and was standing before a statue of the Virgin Mary when she had a vision of the White House. The numerals 1 – 9 – 6 – 0 appeared above it against a dark cloud. A young, blue-eyed man stood

Nostradamus, above, the 16th-century seer, is credited with having prophesied many major world events, among them the recent Gulf War, above left. But many say the predictions are only given credibility with hindsight.

at the door. A voice then told her that a Democrat, who would be inaugurated as President in 1960, would be assassinated while in office.

She predicted Kennedy's brother's death in 1968 – in an even more startling way – while addressing a convention at the Ambassador Hotel, Los Angeles. She invited questions from the floor and someone asked if Robert Kennedy would ever be president. Suddenly, Jeane Dixon saw a black curtain fall between her and the audience, and she told the questioner: 'No, he will not. He will never be President of the United States, because of a tragedy right here in this hotel.' A week later Robert Kennedy was gunned down in that very hotel.

But Jeane Dixon is not always right. In fact, even the best seers claim only a 70 per cent success rate, and sceptics argue that it appears so high only because their predictions are vague.

Jeane Dixon, below, is a modern American seer who predicted the assassinations of both President John F. Kennedy and his brother, Robert, left, as well as civil rights leader, Martin Luther King.

" THERE REMAIN ON RECORD SOME EXTRAORDINARY STORIES OF PREMONITIONS THAT ARE DIFFICULT TO EXPLAIN ACCORDING TO THE LAWS OF CONVENTIONAL SCIENCE – UNLESS THERE IS SOMETHING WRONG WITH OUR CONCEPT OF SPACE AND TIME. **"**

Sceptics, of course, will argue that it is impossible to look into the future, many of them feeling that, until the existence of precognition is proved in the laboratory, it cannot be taken seriously. But, although it may not be easy to look ahead at will, there remain on record some extraordinary stories of premonitions that are difficult to explain according to the laws of conventional science – unless there is something wrong with our concept of space and time.

A first-class example of this is the experience of Mark Twain. Before he became a famous writer – and while he was still known by the name of Samuel Clemens – he worked as an apprentice pilot on a steamboat, the *Pennsylvania*, which plied the Mississippi river. His younger brother, Henry, worked as a clerk on the same boat. Samuel went to visit his sister in St Louis; and, while he was there, had a vivid dream, featuring a metal coffin resting on two chairs. In it was his brother and, resting on his chest, a bouquet of white flowers with a crimson one in the middle.

A few days later, back on the boat, Samuel had an argument with the chief pilot of the *Pennsylvania* and was transferred to another boat, the *Lacey*. His brother, however, stayed aboard the *Pennsylvania*, which was travelling up the river two days ahead of the *Lacey*. When Samuel reached Greenville, Mississippi, he was told that the *Pennsylvania* had blown up just outside Memphis with the loss of 150 lives. His brother Henry, however, was still alive, though badly scalded, and Samuel spent six days and nights with him until he died. Exhausted, he fell into a deep sleep. When he awoke, he found his brother's body had been removed from the room, so he went to find it.

It was just as he had seen it in the dream. Henry was in a metal coffin, which rested on two chairs. But one detail was missing – the flowers. Then, as Samuel watched, an elderly woman entered the room carrying a bouquet of white flowers with a single red rose in the centre. She placed them on Henry's body and left. Mark Twain's glimpse of the future had been fulfilled in practically every detail.

The Mind Science Foundation of Texas carried out an experiment in 1979 to detect whether people could foretell where Skylab would fall to Earth. Very few, however, accurately predicted Australia.

CASEBOOK

A NIGHTMARE COMES TRUE

On the evening of Friday, 26 May 1979, the world was shocked to learn that an American Airlines DC-10 airliner had crashed – a mass of flames and twisted wreckage – on take-off from Chicago's O'Hare International Airport. The lives of 273 people were lost in the worst disaster in the history of flying ever to occur in the United States.

In Cincinnati, Ohio, 23-year-old office manager David Booth sat slumped in horrified disbelief in front of his television. For 10 consecutive nights before the disaster, he had slept through the same terrible nightmare. First, he had heard the sound of engines failing and then looked on helplessly as a huge American Airlines aeroplane swerved sharply, rolled over and crashed to the ground in a mass of red and orange flames. Not only did he see the crash and hear the explosion in his dreams, he also felt the heat of the flames. Each time he awoke in terror and was obsessed all day by the memory of the hideous occurrence. He was sure it was a premonition.

'There was never any doubt to me that something was going to happen,' he said. 'It wasn't like a dream. It was like I was standing

there watching the whole thing – like watching television.'

After several nights, he could no longer keep his terrible premonition to himself; and, on Tuesday, 22 May 1979, he telephoned the Federal Aviation Authority at the Greater Cincinnati Airport. Then he called American Airlines and a psychiatrist at the University of Cincinnati. They listened sympathetically, but that failed to make Booth feel any better. Three days later, almost out of his mind with worry, he heard the news of the DC-10 crash.

The Federal Aviation Authority had taken David Booth's call seriously enough to attempt, in vain, to match up the details of his nightmare with some known airport or aeroplane somewhere in the country. When they heard the news of the crash, of course, the details tallied all too well. 'It was uncanny,' said Jack Barker, public affairs officer for the southern region of the FAA. 'There were differences, but there were many similarities. The greatest similarity was his calling [naming] the airline and the aeroplane ... and that [the plane] came in inverted.' Booth had mentioned a 'three-engine aircraft' resembling a DC-10, and the crash site he described was similar in many aspects to the airport at Chicago.

David Booth stopped having nightmares once the disaster had happened, but he continued to feel disturbed by the whole affair. 'How can you make sense of something like that?' he asked. 'There's no explanation for it. No meaning. No conclusion. It just doesn't make sense.'

ONE OF THE STRANGEST STORIES TO HAVE EMERGED FROM THE CLOUD OF MYSTERY THAT SURROUNDS THE ANCIENT SCIENCE OF ALCHEMY IS THAT OF THE ELUSIVE MODERN MASTER KNOWN AS FULCANELLI. WHAT DID HE ACHIEVE? AND IF HE INDEED DISCOVERED THE ELIXIR OF LIFE, COULD HE STILL BE ALIVE TODAY?

A. E. S. Fulcanelli

The name Fulcanelli has flickered tantalisingly in and out of modern occult literature and speculation for more than half a century. Yet the true identity of the 20th-century alchemist working behind this pseudonym remains to this day a complete mystery.

It was in the early 1920s that the Fulcanelli legend started, as Parisian occultists and alchemists began overhearing oblique and intriguing references to an actual master, alive and working secretly in their midst. These references came mainly from a certain Eugène Canseliet – an intense, slightly-built man in his early twenties who was known to be an enthusiastic researcher into alchemy. They were also bandied about by his constant companion and friend, the impoverished artist and illustrator, Jean-Julien Champagne, who was 22 years Canseliet's senior. The pair, who rented adjacent quarters on the sixth storey of a dilapidated tenement at 59 *bis*, rue de Rochechouart, in the Montmartre district of Paris, had become the focal point of a small, select circle of occultists, and were frequently seen in the city's great libraries – the Arsenal, the Sainte Geneviève, the Mazarin and the Bibliothèque Nationale – poring over rare books and manuscripts.

Those on the periphery of this informal study-group heard hints that the Master Fulcanelli was elderly, distinguished, rich, immensely learned and possibly of aristocratic or noble lineage. He was said to be a genuine, practising alchemist who, if he had not done so already, was on the brink of perfecting 'the Great Work' – the manufacture of the Philosopher's Stone and the Elixir, which could prolong life indefinitely.

But who the Master really was remained unknown. Few had apparently met him – except, so they claimed, Champagne and Canseliet. Certain sceptics even began to question the very fact of his existence.

Then, in the autumn of 1926, evidence of the Master's reality – or at least the reality of someone – appeared. It came in the form of a remarkable

*In*Focus

THE MYSTERY OF THE CATHEDRALS

In his book *Le Mystère des Cathédrales,* Fulcanelli takes the reader on a guided and interpretative tour of many of France's finest examples of Gothic architecture, including the Cathedral of Notre Dame in Paris. Like many mystical commentators before him, he sees architecture as a means of passing on esoteric knowledge, encoded in the form and proportion of a building.

FULCANELLI

The bracket in the mansion of Lallemant in Bourges, top, far left, shows a medieval adept holding the Vessel of the 'Great Work', in which the Elixir of Life is prepared.

Eugène Canseliet and Jean-Julien Champagne, reputedly pupils of the mysterious Fulcanelli, both lived at the house above left.

Marguerite de France (1553-1615), below, is believed by some to have known the secret of the 'Great Work'. Rumour suggested that Fulcanelli might have been descended from her.

His enthusiasm for Gothic architecture is reached via a circuitous route that involved a kind of punning logic. Thus, he interprets Gothic Art, *Art Gothique*, as *argot-hique* – reminding us that *argot* (cant or slang) is defined in dictionaries as 'a language peculiar to all individuals who wish to communicate their thoughts without being understood by outsiders.' Fulcanelli claims that those who use this secret language are descendants of the sailors who accompanied Jason on his search for the Golden Fleece – aboard the ship *Argo*. They, he claims, 'spoke the *langue argotique* [language of the *Argo*]... while they were sailing towards the felicitous shores of Colchos... '

But how does Fulcanelli's method work in practice? In the Portal of the Virgin of Notre Dame Cathedral, *left,* for instance, he sees the medallions of the sarcophagus as symbols of the seven planetary metals. According to standard alchemical interpretation, the Sun stands for gold, Mercury for quicksilver, Saturn for lead, Venus for copper, the Moon for silver, Jupiter for tin and Mars for iron. Taken as a whole, Fulcanelli claims, the portal gives clues as to how to transmute these metals. But Fulcanelli has not made matters too easy, and the final step in interpretation is left to the alchemist. Nevertheless, as Fulcanelli's pupil Canseliet reveals in his introduction to the book: 'The key to the major arcanum is given quite openly in one of the figures.'

book, *Le Mystère des Cathédrales* (The Mystery of the Cathedrals), published in a limited luxury edition of only 300 copies and subtitled *An Esoteric Interpretation of the Hermetic Symbols of the Great Work*. Its preface was by Eugène Canseliet, then aged only 26, and it contained 36 illustrations, two in colour, by the artist Champagne. The text itself was ascribed simply to Fulcanelli. The book purported to interpret the symbolism of various Gothic cathedrals and other buildings in Europe as encoded instructions of alchemical secrets, a concept only darkly hinted at by previous writers on the esoteric in art and architecture. Among occultists, it caused a minor sensation.

In his preface, the young Canseliet intimated that his Master, Fulcanelli – the name is a phonetic approximation of Vulcan, the blacksmith god, and Helios, the Sun-charioteer – had attained the Philosopher's Stone, thereby becoming mystically transfigured and illuminated, and then disappeared. As Canseliet put it: 'He disappeared when the fatal hour struck, when the Sign was accomplished... Fulcanelli is no more. But we have at least this consolation that his thought remains, warm and vital, enshrined for ever in these pages.'

SECRET OF LONGEVITY

Perhaps understandably – especially in view of the immense scholarship and unique haunting qualities of the book – speculation about Fulcanelli's true identity ran wild within the occult fraternity. There were even suggestions that he was a surviving member of the former French royal family, the Valois. Although they were supposed to have died out in 1589 on the demise of Henri III, it was known that members of the family had dabbled in magic and mysticism and that Marguerite de France, daughter of Henri II and wife of Henri IV of Navarre, had survived until 1615. What is more, one of her many lovers was the esoterically inclined Francis Bacon (whom many still claim as an adept to this day). She was divorced in 1599 and her personal crest bore the magical pentagram, each of the five points carrying one letter of the Latin word *salus* – meaning 'health'. So could the reputedly aristocratic Fulcanelli be a descendant of the Valois, and did the Latin motto hint that some important alchemical secret of longevity had been passed on to him by the family? These were, at least, possibilities.

But there were other, more or less plausible identifications. Some claimed Fulcanelli was the bookseller-occultist, Pierre Dujols; and that, together with his wife, he ran a shop in the rue de Rennes in the Luxembourg district of Paris. But Dujols was already known to have been only a speculative alchemist, writing under the *nom de plume* of Magophon. It seemed unlikely he would hide behind two aliases. Another suggestion was that Fulcanelli was the writer J.H. Rosny, the Elder. Yet this author's life was too well-known to the public for the theory to find general acceptance.

There were in fact three practising alchemists in Paris at around this period, operating under the respective pseudonyms of Auriger, Faugerons and Dr Jaubert. But the argument against any of them being Fulcanelli was much the same as that against Dujols-Magophon: why use more than one alias?

Finally, there were Eugène Canseliet and Jean-Julien Champagne themselves, both of whom were directly connected with Fulcanelli's book, and both of whom claimed to have known the Master Fulcanelli personally.

But the argument against Canseliet's identification as the Master was fairly straightforward: he was far too young to have acquired the erudition and knowledge so obviously and remarkably demonstrated by the text of *Le Mystère des Cathédrales*. And a study of his preface showed a distinct difference in style from that of the text, a difference that remains notable in Canseliet's later writings.

Champagne seemed, at least to some, the more likely contender. He was older and more experienced, and his work as an artist could have taken him around the various cathedrals, châteaux and other curious monuments imbued with symbolism that Fulcanelli had obviously studied and interpreted in great detail as keys to the 'Great Work'.

On the other hand, Champagne was a noted braggart, practical joker, punster and drunkard, who

Eugène Canseliet, above, claimed to be a pupil of Fulcanelli but did not reveal his identity.

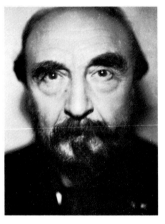

Many suspected that the writer J. H. Rosny the Elder (1856-1940), above, was the figure behind the pseudonym 'Fulcanelli'.

Jean-Julien Champagne, left – artist and illustrator, and constant companion of Fulcanelli's supposed pupil Eugène Canseliet – was a braggart and practical joker. His habit of trying to pass himself off as Fulcanelli added to the confusion about the true identity of the master alchemist.

frequently liked to pass himself off as Fulcanelli – although his behaviour was entirely out of keeping with the traditional solemn oath of the adept that promises he will remain anonymous and let his written work speak for itself.

Two examples of Champagne's wicked sense of humour suffice to show the great gap between his own way of thinking and that of the noble-minded author of *Le Mystère des Cathédrales*. Champagne once persuaded a gullible young follower that he should stock up with a massive supply of coal to ensure that his alchemical furnace was constantly burning at the required temperature. The naïve youth lugged sack after sack of the fuel up to his garret until there was barely room in which to lie down and sleep. Champagne then announced to the would-be alchemist that the quest was an utterly vain and dangerous one – leaving him almost banished from his apartment by coal and, presumably, considerably out of pocket into the bargain.

FAKE LETTER

Another carefully contrived prank of Champagne involved the forging of a letter, purportedly from Paul le Cour, who edited and published a periodical called *Atlantis*, to the publisher of the *Mercure de France*. In it, the fake le Cour urged the setting up of a fund by the *Mercure's* subscribers to build a monument for the victims of the fabled lost continent – a cenotaph that, since he suggested it be placed in the middle of the Sargasso Sea, would have to be unsinkable. Champagne sat back and laughed while the unsuspecting 'real' le Cour received an indignant volley from the publisher of the *Mercure*.

To crown all of this, Jean-Julien Champagne's huge and almost insatiable appetite for absinthe and Pernod finally killed him. The poor artist died in 1932, of gangrene, in his sixth-floor garret, his friend Eugène Canseliet having nursed him through his long, painful and particularly unpleasant illness. (Champagne's toes actually fell off before his death at the age of only 55.)

Only three years earlier, a second work by the mysterious Fulcanelli had been published. This appeared under the title *Les Demeures Philosophales* (The Dwellings of the Philosophers). It was issued in two volumes and was double the length of the first book. Like its predecessor, it interpreted particular architectural embellishments, such as ornate ceiling panels – this time, in 12th- to 15th-century mansions and châteaux – as encoded alchemical secret knowledge.

The appearance of this book inspired yet another theory about Fulcanelli's possible identity. Inside the rear cover of the second volume were the armorial bearings of Dom Robert Jollivet, a 13th-century abbot of Mont St-Michel, known to have dabbled in alchemy. This, according to one theory, implied that the name of Jollivet was intended to indicate that his modern near-namesake, F. Jolivet Castelot, was in fact Fulcanelli. Jolivet Castelot was President of the Alchemists' Society of France from around 1914 and also a prominent member of the *Ordre Kabbalistique de la Rose-Croix*. Between 1896 and 1935, he had published many studies in hermeticism, alchemy and spagyrics – the art of

Some believed that F. Jolivet Castelot, below, was in fact Fulcanelli. But he said he was a practising 'archimist' – someone who tries to use ordinary chemical methods to transmute base metals into gold – rather than an alchemist.

making special concoctions using alchemical principles. But he made no secret of the fact that he was an 'archimist' rather than an alchemist – that is, a researcher who tries to effect transmutation by orthodox chemistry, rather than a more mystically inclined alchemist.

There was, however, an even stranger heraldic shield on the final page of the original edition of *Le Mystère des Cathedrales*. The occult scholar Robert Ambelain – who, in the 1930s, made one of the most thorough investigations into the Fulcanelli mystery – was the first to draw attention to this shield. Among many other alleged clues, Ambelain pointed out that the dog-Latin motto beneath the shield was *uber campa agna*, a phonetic approximation of Hubert Champagne. And, he claimed, Hubert was the middle name of the artist, Jean-Julien Champagne. He also noted that the pseudonym Fulcanelli is an anagram of *l'écu finale* (the final shield), indirectly indicating the heraldic device and its motto.

Eugène Canseliet, however, flatly and consistently denied the identification of Champagne as Fulcanelli – or of anyone else, for that matter. Furthermore, Hubert was not the artist's middle name, he claimed – although it is, by sheer coincidence, that of his own maternal grandfather. In any case, he further asserted, the damning shield was inserted into the first edition of the book by Champagne without the permission or knowledge of the Master Fulcanelli, or of himself – as another of his practical jokes.

DECEPTIONS AND FORGERIES

Canseliet, who claimed to be Fulcanelli's sole surviving pupil, similarly claimed that an inscription on Champagne's gravestone, along with a deliberate forgery of Fulcanelli's signature by the artist, were further attempts to deceive or mislead. The epitaph, at the cemetery of Arnouvilles-les-Gonesses, reads:

'Here rests Jean-Julien Champagne
Apostolicus Hermeticae Scientiae
1877-1932.'

Another alleged Fulcanelli signature, meanwhile, also appeared in a handwritten dedication of the original edition of *Le Mystère des Cathedrales*, which was given by Champagne to an occultist named Jules Boucher. It was signed A.H.S. Fulcanelli – the same initials as those of the Latin motto on the gravestone of Champagne at Arnouvilles-les-Gonesses. And, interestingly, in Jules Boucher's *Manual of Magic*, the author's dedication is to 'My Master Fulcanelli' .

Curiously enough, despite all his alleged evidence to the contrary, Ambelain reaches the conclusion that Champagne actually did achieve the Philosopher's Stone – the stone that transmutes base metals into gold and allows the manufacture of the Elixir of Life – some three years before his dreadful death.

But if Ambelain is correct, how could this explain Champagne's untimely death through over-indulgence in drink at the age of just 55?

And yet, more than one person has attested to Fulcanelli's success in transmutation, in his perfection of the 'Great Work', and his continued existence even into the 1990s – which would make him more than 140 years old!

> **"** THE LEADING ALCHEMISTS IN CHINA DECIDED THAT THE PHILOSOPHER'S STONE WAS RED CINNABAR (MERCURIAL SULFIDE). ONE SAID THAT THIS, COMBINED WITH HONEY, AND TAKEN FOR A YEAR, WOULD RESTORE YOUTH AND ENABLE THE INDIVIDUAL TO FLY. TAKEN FOR MORE THAN A YEAR, IT WOULD CONFER IMMORTALITY. **"**
>
> STAN GOOCH,
> CITIES OF DREAMS

Could the inscription on Jean-Julien Champagne's gravestone, below, have been a last attempt to convince people that he was the mysterious alchemist?

Joanna Southcott, left, made the amazing claim – in late middle age – that she was pregnant with 'the Lamb' (or Messiah). Presumably, she had astonishing charisma in order to persuade several thousands of followers that she was, indeed, a channel for divine revelation.

KNOWN FOR A WHOLE RANGE
OF BIZARRE BELIEFS, THE
19TH-CENTURY DEVON
PROPHET JOANNA SOUTHCOTT
STILL HAS A SMALL, BUT
FERVENT, FOLLOWING

JOANNA SOUTHCOTT – NOTORIOUS PROPHET

While Joanna Southcott's milder critics called her an 'enthusiast', her enemies referred to her as a 'fanatic'. Her family, however, simply thought her mad. It is hardly surprising: neither she nor her principal disciples ever achieved anything they promised to do. Yet such was the personality of the former Devon milkmaid that, when she claimed to be pregnant with the 'new Messiah' in 1814, the cream of London society showered her with expensive gifts. And nearly 50 years after her death, with her prophecy of the coming of the 'second Jesus Christ' unfulfilled, one of her more extreme disciples was still able to build a mansion costing £10,000 from the offerings of 'Southcottians' in Melbourne, Australia, alone – subscriptions that would have been worth about £1 million today. Even nowadays, around the world, small but active groups of followers continue to await the opening of her enigmatic sealed box. This, they believe, contains the secret of world peace, happiness, and the millennium, as foretold in the *Book of Revelation*.

Joanna Southcott, the unlikely centre of all this spiritual speculation, was born in the hamlet of Gittisham, Devon, and baptised in the parish church of Ottery St Mary on 6 June 1750. Her father,

The cartoon, below, dating from 1814, is entitled Joanna Southcott, the prophetess, excommunicating the bishops. Southcott is depicted as the archetypal man-hater, uttering the line: 'I put no more trust in bishops than men.' She believed all normal, sexual, or even romantic associations beneath her; only God was good enough to make her pregnant.

William, was a small tenant farmer of moderate religious beliefs; and her mother, who died when Joanna was a small girl, was a devout Wesleyan. Both mother and daughter were, according to William Southcott, 'too religious by far'.

Despite Joanna's fanatical church-going, her early years were normal enough. While tending her father's cattle, she even had a passionate love affair with Noah Bishop, a neighbouring farmer's son and friend of her brother Joseph, who helped the couple to keep their liaison secret.

GROWING MAD

At the age of 20, she moved to Honiton, Devon, to work as a shop girl, rejecting several suitors as beneath her – although some, at least, were property owners. By now, she was already developing the obsession that her body was too good for mortal men, referring to herself as the 'temple of Shiloh', the legendary sanctuary of the Ark of the Covenant. She also caused a minor domestic scandal when employed as a maid in a country house, claiming that a footman had molested her. But the footman denied the charge, telling his employer – who believed him – that Joanna was 'growing mad'.

Whatever the truth of the matter, the footman's claim seemed to have some foundation, for Joanna wrote later that 'divine command' had brought about her dismissal so that she could move to the county town of Exeter, where she was to work as a shop girl in an upholstering establishment for the next 20 years. Her employer later testified that, during this time, her 'character was blameless and her service faithful'. For, all these years, she shunned the society of men and spent most of her spare time at church and chapel.

Every Sunday, she went to communion twice, attending an early service in her parish church and a later morning service at the cathedral, while spending the afternoons and evenings at the local Wesleyan chapel.

At Christmas 1791, she became a full member of the Wesleyan congregation. It was to be a short and unhappy association. On Easter Monday 1792, the 42-year-old convert interrupted the Bible class. She had, she announced, been 'sent by God to Exeter' 20 years before to reveal to the world that she was 'the Lamb's wife' and would henceforth be his earthly representative.

'The announcement was not well received,' according to a contemporary account. 'There was uproar and cries of "shame" and "blasphemy" in the room, while Joanna fell into a fever and fits.'

Sympathetic members of the congregation carried the writhing figure across country to the home of her sister, Mrs Carter, at Plympton. For 10 days, Joanna lay in delirium – or, as she later described it, 'struggling with the powers of darkness'. Then she awoke and began writing 'prophecies' in rambling prose and doggerel rhyme.

There was never anything profound about the prophecies of Joanna Southcott – except perhaps her final foretelling of the impending 'birth of the second Christ'. Her 'prophecies' were either vague generalities concerning famine, war and pestilence at some time in the future, or particular omens and warnings that might or might not have meaning for an individual.

I'll well Dust their Woolsacks and make them drunk in my fury; I will bring down their strength to the earth.

Lay it on hip and thigh. Brave Tonzer Smile the unbelievers. I put no more trust in Bishops as men. than I do in their Chariots and Horses but my trust is the Lord of Hosts

To Book of Wonders

PHETESS EXCOMMUNICATING THE BISHOPS
off, having already cut off Four Bishops for refusing to hear her Visitation.

Joanna Southcott spent much of her free time in devotional studies at Exeter Cathedral, right. Indeed, she was to announce to the local Wesleyan congregation that she had been 'sent by God to Exeter' to reveal to the world that she was to be 'the Lamb's wife'. When the cries of 'shame' and 'blasphemy' became unbearable, she promptly had convulsions.

Certainly, the majority of her specific prophecies failed to materialise. One of the first examples was that the quality of the harvest for 1792 would be 'so bad that the best wheat would not fetch four shillings and sixpence a bushel'.

When her sister, Mrs Carter, read this in her farmhouse, surrounded by the nicely ripening corn, she wrote to their father echoing the opinion of the footman all those years previously: 'Joanna,' she said, 'is growing out of her senses.'

SEALED PROPHECIES

In fact, Joanna was only just getting into her stride. In her days as a shop girl, she had been sweeping up one day when she found a small oval seal bearing the initials 'I.C.' with two small stars. She decided that this was divinely sent – 'I.C.' meaning 'Iesus Christus' – and, with it, she began to seal up bundles of her prophecies to be opened at a future time as a test of her abilities. She wrote to every clergyman in Devon, from bishops to curates, demanding recognition. Then, in 1798, she moved to Bristol where, two years later, she published a booklet, *The Strange Effects of Faith,* inviting 'any twelve ministers' to try her claims. It was an unimpressive document at first sight – the printer's bill included the item: 'For correcting the spelling and grammar of the prophecies, 2/6d.'

By a strange chance, the Southcott publication coincided with the incarceration in the lunatic asylum at Islington, North London, of another 'prophet', Richard Brothers, a former naval lieutenant whose own lurid claims had attracted the attentions of King George III himself. Discharged on half pay after completing 13 years' meritorious service, Brothers had decided that the loyal oath required for him to continue collecting his pay was blasphemous, and wrote to the King, Speaker, and Members of the House of Commons in 1791, demanding that he be proclaimed by the House 'the nephew of the Almighty'. In his letter, he forecast – accurately – the forthcoming violent deaths of the King of Sweden, Gustavus III, and Louis XVI of France, as a result of which his book, *A Revealed*

The design of Joanna's 'seal', copied from one she had found in the shop where she had worked as a young girl, is shown above. She took the initials 'I.C.' to stand for 'Iesus Christus'.

Richard Brothers, above right, was the self-appointed 'Prince of Hebrews and Ruler of the World'. King George III was so annoyed by Brothers' ravings that he had him put away in an asylum. Yet such was the general willingness to believe in anything prophetic that Brothers' cause actually helped further that of Joanna Southcott.

RICHARD BROTHERS PRINCE OF THE HEBREWS

Knowledge of Prophecies and Times, published in 1794, enjoyed brisk sales. But one of its 'prophecies' claimed that, on 19 November 1795, he would be 'revealed as Prince of Hebrews and Ruler of the World'. This so upset King George – himself the victim of bouts of insanity – that, on 4 March 1795, Brothers was arrested by two King's Messengers on a royal warrant issued by the Duke of Portland. After being examined by the Privy Council, he was thrown into Islington asylum.

Despite such manifest eccentricities, Brothers had attracted a considerable number of converts, one of them William Sharp, a well-to-do engraver, who had made sufficient money to build a house in Chiswick from the proceeds of such best-selling pictures as *Hector, The Old Tower Lion,* a portrait of John Hunter the pioneering surgeon, and copperplate versions of paintings by Reynolds and Gainsborough. Just before Brothers' arrest, Sharp had published a portrait of him as the 'Prince of

Hebrews', with rays of heavenly light radiating from his head. The portrait was dedicated to Brothers from 'a true and devout believer'.

All his life, Sharp seemed to need to believe in philosophical and religious novelties. He had been a friend and admirer of Tom Paine, author of *The Rights of Man,* before being converted to the ideas of Mesmer and Swedenborg, and finally to those of Lieutenant Brothers. Now, with Brothers safely locked away, Sharp read Joanna Southcott's booklet and became interested in the new 'prophetess'.

In January 1802, Sharp – accompanied by three respectable Church of England rectors (Stanhope Bruce of Inglesham, Wiltshire, Thomas Foley of Old Swinford, Worcestershire, and Thomas Webster of Oakington, Cambridgeshire) and three other gentlemen – visited Joanna and held what was to become known as the 'First Trial' of her sealed writings at the Guildhall, Exeter. When the seals were broken,

each man found something in the writings that seemed to have a profound bearing on himself; and at the end of the session, all acclaimed Southcott as a 'true prophet'. For her part, she welcomed them as her 'Seven Stars'.

Public recognition by seven such respectable figures helped the Southcott cause immensely; and at Sharp's suggestion, she moved to London. In May 1802, she settled into High House, Paddington, and received growing audiences, many of whom came to mock but remained to pray. Perhaps her popularity lay in the scarcity of female prophets, plus her own undoubted personal magnetism. But apart from an emphasis on universal brotherly love, there was nothing revolutionary about her general teachings. In the spring of 1805, an Exeter-born 'dissenting' minister named William Tozer, who opened the first 'Southcottian Chapel' at Duke Street, Southwark, London, even used an orthodox Anglican prayer book.

But after a short while at Paddington, Joanna became increasingly convinced that she personally was the one vehicle of salvation. At Exeter, she had caused trouble by describing herself as 'the Lamb's wife'. In October 1802, she was more specific: 'I am bringing forth to the world a spiritual man,' she declared, 'the second Jesus Christ.'

▟▟ EVEN NOWADAYS, AROUND THE WORLD, SMALL BUT ACTIVE GROUPS OF FOLLOWERS CONTINUE TO AWAIT THE OPENING OF HER ENIGMATIC SEALED BOX. THIS, THEY BELIEVE, CONTAINS THE SECRET OF WORLD PEACE... ▟▟

PERSPECTIVES

THE NEW MOSES

The Southcottians are considered by those who know of them to be frankly odd. The Church of Jesus Christ of Latter Day Saints (Mormons) also believes its leader to be a prophet, but is increasingly considered to be part of the Establishment.

It was not always so. After the martyrdom of the first 'prophet', Joseph Smith, in 1844, his successor, Brigham Young – 'the new Moses' – led the faithful away from persecution to 'the promised land'. They had no idea where they were going but still they followed this tough and charismatic man thousands of miles across America, until he suddenly pointed at an expanse of inhospitable salt flats. 'This is the place,' he declared. 'The desert shall blossom as a rose.' Against all the odds, it did; and the Mormon centre of Salt Lake City was founded there.

By 1873, when the print of Salt Lake City, *right,* was made, the community of Mormons had grown considerably, spreading out across the landscape. Today, Salt Lake City is the state capital of the American state of Utah.

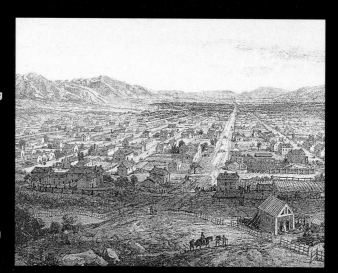

WHEN JOANNA SOUTHCOTT ANNOUNCED SHE WAS PREGNANT WITH THE MESSIAH, SHE WAS 64. BUT THE ECCENTRIC CLAIMS SHE MADE AT THE END OF HER LIFE WERE AS NOTHING COMPARED WITH THOSE MADE BY LATER 'PROPHETS'

As Joanna Southcott's idiosyncratic ministry gained momentum, her pronouncements became increasingly bizarre. Eternal salvation would be the lot of only 144,000 souls; moreover, to gain admittance to heaven, her followers would have to be 'sealed' by her. She therefore began issuing what amounted to share certificates for a stake in paradise.

These certificates were half-page printed sheets reading: 'The sealed of the Lord – the elect precious man's redemption – to inherit the tree of life – to be made heirs of God and joint-heirs with Jesus Christ – Joanna Southcott.' The impression of her oval seal with its stars and the initials I.C. (Iesus Christus) was appended in red wax at the bottom of each certificate.

By 1805, when 10,000 of these certificates had been issued, Joanna was accused, probably falsely, of selling them; but even if the accusations were true, the bottom fell dramatically out of the market in 1809, when a particularly brutal murderess, named Mary Bateman, was hanged publicly at York and – embarrassingly for Joanna's movement – was found to be a certificate-holder.

In any case, money was plentifully forthcoming from other sources. In 1803, a second 'trial' – or public debate – of Joanna's prophecies was held before a wealthy invited audience at High House, Joanna's home in Paddington, London. Nearly 60 people received 'personal messages' when the sealed documents were opened and read out, and all of those attending the debate made handsome offerings. Another source of income was the second Southcottian chapel opened at Bermondsey, east London, the same year. Here, an apprentice, Henry

The contemporary cartoon, above, entitled The impostor or obstetric dispute, *shows the ridicule afforded by 64-year-old Joanna Southcott's announcement that she was carrying 'Shiloh' – the new Messiah, who would be born on Christmas Day. Oddly, eminent doctors agreed that she showed all the symptoms of pregnancy which, had it run its natural course, would have ended with the birth of a child on 25 December, 1814. Sympathizers showered her and the unborn child with gifts such as these, left, including – somewhat incongruously – a Bible, with which a Messiah would surely be familiar.*

PROPHECIES OF A NEW MESSIAH

The Southcott 'seal', above, was appended to certificates issued by the prophetess to the 144,000 souls lucky enough to be approved by her to gain admittance to paradise. There was a rumour that a place in paradise could be bought, but the bottom fell out of the market when a notorious murderess was found to be a certificate-holder.

The elegant crystal goblets, right, were used by the Southcottians for their communion services and were a gift from a wealthy believer. Yet more funds helped establish chapels, such as that in Bermondsey, London, below.

'Joseph the Dreamer' Prescott, and his spiritual manager, Elias Carpenter, 'dreamed' for the benefit of the poorer classes of London. And the working classes of northern England were catered for in the autumn when Joanna went to Salford, Leeds and Stockton-on-Tees, setting up chapels in each town. A third and final 'trial' of her writings took place before a packed crowd in December 1804. Thereafter, to all intents and purposes 'Southcottism' finally became an established, if eccentric, part of English religious life.

At the height of Joanna Southcott's popularity, the 'prophet' Richard Brothers was released, a broken man, from the lunatic asylum at Islington, north London, and went to live quietly in St John's Wood. As both prophets had attracted the attention of the wealthy engraver William Sharp, Joanna's name had been linked with that of Brothers, although they had never met. Joanna's personal ambitions knew

no bounds, however. Now she spent two days carefully defacing as many as 1,000 copies of Sharp's engraving of Brothers as the 'Prince of Hebrews', only to order Sharp to make a similarly dramatic engraving of herself in January 1812, for distribution among the faithful.

Her next public move, too, echoed that of Brothers 18 years before – but was, if anything, more extreme. In the late summer of 1813, she wrote personal letters to every bishop, peer, and Member of Parliament, as well as messages to *The Times* and *Morning Herald*, announcing that she would shortly become 'the mother of Shiloh'.

'In ten years from the fourth of the century,' she said, 'the Messiah will come.' On 13 October 1813,

she retired permanently from public life to her house at 38 Manchester Street, Manchester Square, in London's West End, with two female disciples, Jane Townley and Ann Underwood.

In late March 1814 – 'ten years from the fourth of the century' – news leaked out that the prophetess was ill, but it was not until 1 August that Jane Townley called for the assistance of nine prominent medical men. They included Dr Joseph Adams, editor of the *Medical and Physical Journal*, Richard Reece, a leading fellow of the Royal College of Physicians, and Dr John Sims, a fellow of the Royal Society and a noted scientific polymath.

It was Dr Adams who issued a cautious statement about Joanna's health to the press on behalf of himself and his colleagues. Joanna Southcott was now 64 years old; but, he confessed, in a

Dr Richard Reece, top, was one of the medical men who confessed themselves bewildered by Joanna Southcott's 'pregnancy' at the age of 64. It was to Dr Reece that Joanna finally announced that, instead of giving birth to the Messiah, she was 'gradually dying', although he could find nothing wrong with her. Yet, only a few days later, she was dead.

The Rev. George Turner of Leeds, above, took over the Southcottian movement after Joanna's death.

younger woman, her symptoms would indicate a pregnancy of four months. If such a pregnancy were to run its course, the child would be born on Christmas Day.

Not unnaturally, the news caused a sensation at every level of society. Medical aspects of the case were discussed avidly in the better newspapers and journals, while gifts of money, jewellery and clothing poured in to Manchester Street. In September, a crib costing £200 was made to order by Seddons of Aldersgate, a leading furniture company, and £100 was spent on a set of silver 'pap-spoons'; while–somewhat superfluously, perhaps, if the child were to be the Messiah – a richly bound vellum Bible, hand tooled and blocked in gold leaf, was sent to await the birth.

On 19 November, however, when Dr Reece called to examine her, Joanna announced that she was 'gradually dying'. As far as Reece could see, she was in good health, but nevertheless she insisted on giving him written instructions to 'open her body' four days after her death, and over the next few weeks all the gifts for 'Shiloh' were returned.

On Christmas Day, growing weak, she gave her last instructions to her female companions: her body was to be 'kept warm' until the post-mortem. And on 27 December, Joanna Southcott died. On New Year's Eve, Dr Reece performed the autopsy, watched by Dr Adams and Dr Sims, and later published a pamphlet of his findings. As far as he had been able to tell, there had been no physical 'pregnancy' and there was no functional disorder or organic disease in the body. Probably all the mischief lay in the brain, which was not examined owing to the high degree of putrefaction – hastened, of course, by the blazing fires kept going in the house on Joanna's final instructions. It was, apparently, a classic case of hysterical pregnancy, but one that, had it run its course, would – in view of Joanna's claims – have been timed with uncanny accuracy.

GREATER THINGS IN STORE

On New Year's Day 1815, Joanna was buried privately at St John's Wood cemetery, not far from the spot where Richard Brothers, her old rival, was to be interred 10 years later. On her tombstone were engraved the words: 'Thou wilt appear in greater power.'

After Joanna's death, her 'movement' was taken over by George Turner, minister of the Southcottian chapel at Leeds, who was assisted by Jane Townley. Their belief was quite unshaken by the non-appearance of Joanna's promised messianic offspring 'Shiloh'. She had, after all, promised that he would be a 'spiritual man' and, reasoned Turner, this 'spirit' could have entered into any one of Joanna's followers. According to the Bible, a 'prophet is without honour in his own country'; but it would be unforgivable of the Southcottians not to recognize him when he did arrive. In effect, therefore, the title was open to all comers.

One of the first to claim it was Mary Boon, an illiterate who, like Joanna, came from Devon. Her prophecies were written out for her by John Ward, a Baptist lay preacher who had joined Boon when she began to prophesy in 1818, four years after Joanna's death. It was Ward, in fact, who was next to be acclaimed as Joanna's 'Shiloh', though George Turner and Jane Townley were suspicious of him. Ward had been born – significantly, some might think – on Christmas Day 1781 in Cork.

At 12, he was an apprentice shipwright in Bristol with a drink problem, but his alcoholism did not prevent him distinguishing himself on *HMS Blanche* at the battle of Copenhagen in 1801. When he was paid off two years later, he gave up drink, married, and became a shoemaker – and turned to religion. Brought up as a Calvinist, he was next attracted to the Methodists and then to the Baptists, finally taking up with Mary Boon. In 1826, he pronounced himself 'illuminated by the Lord', and declared himself to be Joanna's promised 'Shiloh', though he was popularly known as 'Zion' Ward. His wife, neglected and without income, pronounced him mad and brought him before a magistrate who committed Ward to the workhouse.

When Ward was released, he and a companion, Charles William Twort, evolved a new method of prophecy, divining meanings not only from the words of the King James Bible but also from the actual shape of the print. Their enthusiasm gained them not only followers but 18 months in Derby jail for blasphemy, a punishment that was so unpopular that Parliament debated it and finally cut the sentences short. Ward, described as 'gentle, modest, with a high moral tone' and the preacher of 'spiritual pantheism', died on 12 March 1837, already eclipsed by his more vigorous rival, John Wroe.

RAVING HUNCHBACK

Wroe, a year younger than Ward, was the sickly son of a farmer from Bowling, near Bradford, Yorkshire. As a boy, he had carried a window stone up to the second floor of his father's house, damaged his back and 'was never straight again'. In later years, his hunchback lent his ranting sermons an extra aura of wildness.

Two years after Joanna Southcott's death, in 1816, the first signs of mania appeared in Wroe, who was by this time established as a farmer and woolcomber, although he was very much in debt. He took to reading the Bible as he tramped through his fields, saw visions, fell into spontaneous trances and suffered temporary phases of – presumably hysterical – blindness.

In about 1820, he paid a visit to George Turner's chapel at Leeds; but strangely, although Turner looked suspiciously on gentle John Ward, he was impressed by the wild-eyed Wroe. When Turner died in September 1821, Wroe took over his duties as 'Southcottian' leader, and the movement almost instantly fell foul of the law.

Wroe's peculiarities grew more noticeable as time passed. First, he ordered the Southcottians to discard the names of the months, numbering them instead. Then, he began to grow his beard, demanding that all his male disciples do likewise. He also made two highly publicized attempts to walk on water. When his attempts failed hilariously, he hastily announced that he had been undergoing 'public baptism'.

Certainly, Wroe had the courage of his strange convictions. On 17 April, 1823, he was publicly circumcised at a meeting of believers. But the incident had tragic repercussions. One of his disciples, Henry Lees of Ashton, circumcised an infant called Daniel Grimshaw, who bled to death.

Wroe's trial came about as a result of his sexual tendencies, although the charge of 'swindler' was also levelled at him. In 1827, a 12-year-old girl, Martha Whitley, accused him of having had intercourse with her. At first, Wroe denied the charge; but when, three years later, three more young girls accused him of sexual interference during 'cleansing' ceremonies, he was called to answer.

However, after the trial – an unruly proceeding by all accounts – 'a very considerable number of [the Southcottians] left him and shaved off their beards', including Henry Lees, the over-enthusiastic circumciser. Wroe was never welcome in Ashton again – although, for 40 years afterwards, many of his followers were to be found in the town.

The charge of swindling was almost certainly true. In 1856, Wroe ordered his followers to wear gold rings; but although they paid for the gold, the rings were actually brass. And in 1842, when his printing shop at Wrenthorpe, Wakefield, was broken into by burglars, Wroe's perjury convicted three innocent people, a fact that came to light only when the real culprits were caught, five years later.

Wroe's final prophecy had the same germ of truth as that of Joanna Southcott. In the 1840s, he had forecast that the Millennium would begin in 1863 – but on 5 February of that year, he died suddenly after breaking his collarbone, at Collingwood, Melbourne, Australia, and is buried there.

No portrait exists of Wroe for, unlike Southcott, he thought such things sinful. Possibly his appearance had something to do with the omission, for he was described as having a 'savage, haggard look', with a 'hump back and very prominent nose'.

'There must have been a strange fascination about the man', wrote a late-Victorian commentator, 'for his utterances are but fatuous insipidities with a Biblical twang, having neither the pathetic earnestness of Joanna Southcott, nor the crude originality of her other improver, John Ward.'

*In*FOCUS

JOANNA SOUTHCOTT'S BOX

The whereabouts of Joanna Southcott's mysterious box remains a secret, but it is said to contain important writings that would guide the Church on to new and wiser paths. Moreover, it should be opened by a convocation of bishops. In 1927, psychical researcher Harry Price claimed to have been given a key to the box. It contained, he said, only an old nightcap, a flintlock pistol and various other oddments. He therefore believed the box to be a hoax. Her supporters maintain, however, that whatever Price opened, it was not Joanna's box.

Crime and banditry, the distress of nations and perplexity are still said by Joanna Southcott's followers to continue until her box of sealed writings is opened by the bishops or their representatives. Indeed, they quote, somewhat enigmatically, from *Revelations* in this connection, as follows: 'And the temple of God was opened... and there was seen the Ark [Chart or Box] of his Testament [or Will]... And round about the Throne were four-and-twenty... Elders [Bishops] sitting... and they fall down and cast their crowns [their Wisdom] before the throne... '

A MIRACLE IN TIBET

experience a communication from Mohammed; a secular poet may find himself for an instant at one with the Universe and spend the rest of his life trying to express the glory of that moment's insight.

Such experiences can be used as propaganda for this or that form of belief. But the fact that they are shared by individuals of so many faiths and non-faiths surely means that they cannot be accepted as evidence for one particular form of truth.

The story of Peter's miraculous escape from prison, when chained between two guards (*Acts 12*), is one that even many Christians find difficult to accept. Yet a 20th-century Christian, Sadhu Sundar Singh, not only claimed to have had a similar experience but also spoke of witnessing an extraordinary vision, one that was to change his life.

Sundar Singh's story begins in India, in the early 1890s, when he was still a young boy growing up in a wealthy Sikh family. His mother, a deeply religious woman, had taken Sundar to visit a *sadhu*, a holy man who had chosen the life of a homeless wanderer in search of truth. The meeting between the young boy and the old mystic had a profound effect on Sundar, and he at once made it his resolve to search for God. When he was 14, his quest was intensified by the deaths of his mother and elder brother. A year later, possibly as a result of the missionary influences that were prevalent in India at the time, he struck out against western religion. Christianity was anathema to him; and to show his hatred, he stoned local Christian preachers and publicly burned *The Bible* in his village.

Three days after this denouncement, Sundar is said to have received the sign he had been so fervently looking for. After praying all night, he had a vision. In the vision, Jesus Christ appeared to him

IT SEEMED AS IF SADHU SUNDAR SINGH'S FATE WAS SEALED WHEN HE WAS SENTENCED TO DIE IN A DEEP, DRY WELL — BUT, MIRACULOUSLY, HE SURVIVED

All faiths have their saints, mystics and visionaries who have experiences expressed to them in the vocabulary of their own culture. A Roman Catholic may see a vision of the Virgin Mary; a Quaker may receive a revelation from the 'inner light'; a Muslim may

It was meeting a figure, such as the Indian holy man, right, that was to start the young Sundar Singh on his search for God.

Sadhu Sundar Singh, left, was undaunted by the bleak terrain of the Himalayas, below, and by the hostile reception committee he knew would be waiting for him when he crossed to Tibet.

and said in Hindustani: 'How long will you persecute me? I have come to save you. You pray to know the right way. Take it.'

Sundar's search had ended; and no one was more surprised than he that it should end with a revelation from a Christian God.

This was only the beginning of Sundar's story: with his personal quest now over, a new journey of evangelism had begun. He was baptised into the Christian Church in 1905; but, after taking an Anglican ordination course, he decided that the conventional priesthood was not for him. His newfound faith was not a fragile thing, but then neither was his sense of Indian culture and tradition. Sundar believed he could spread his own vision of Christ only if he remained unfettered by denominational bonds: not for him the dog-collars and suits that he had seen other converted Indian priests wearing. Nor was he willing to block out his awareness of the ever-present spirit world, a world also close to the hearts of some of the villagers among whom he lived and later preached.

To resolve his dilemma, he took the unique step of becoming a Christian *sadhu*, preaching the Gospel without material resources and relying on charity. As such, he was allowed access to areas

*In*Focus

GOOD LORD DELIVER US

Acts 12: 1-17 relates a miracle that has no apparent rational explanation. Peter was imprisoned during one of Herod's anti-Christian purges. Chained between two soldiers, he was awoken in the night by a light in his cell. An angel appeared before him, struck off his chains and led him to freedom – bolts, bars and locks proving no obstacle.

'And the angel said unto him, Gird thyself, and bind on thy sandals. And so he did. And he saith unto him, Cast my garment about thee, and follow me.' Peter 'came to himself' in the city street. Until then, he thought he had been dreaming; but, finding his experience to be real, he went to the home of his friend where a girl, hearing his voice, reported that it was his spirit outside the house. When Peter's friends saw him, they were amazed by his account of his escape.

Nearly 2,000 years later, Sundar Singh's miraculous escape was to cause similar surprise and disbelief.

" ONE THING, HOWEVER, SUSTAINED HIM. WHEN HE HAD FIRST SEEN HIS VISION OF CHRIST, HE REPORTED EXPERIENCING A STRONG SENSE OF PEACE AND JOY . . . THAT FEELING STAYED WITH HIM THROUGHOUT THE DURATION OF HIS INCARCERATION IN THE WELL. **"**

that would have otherwise been closed to him; and as an Indian holy man, albeit a Christian one, he was less likely to alienate the very people he was trying to convert.

Sadhu Sundar Singh made it his special business to evangelise in Tibet. And it was in that strange and mysterious country that the miracle is said to have taken place. He crossed the Himalayas several times on foot and, though it was not easy to make converts in a Buddhist country, his zeal remained undiminished. It was during one of these trips that he was arrested and condemned to death for preaching Christianity.

DEATH SENTENCE

Buddhist law forbids a true disciple to kill, so criminals are executed in ways that, by means of legal fictions, exonerate Buddhists from direct responsibility. Sundar's death sentence could have taken a variety of forms. One method was to sew the victim into a water-saturated bullock's skin: the skin would then be put out to dry, and as it slowly contracted, so the person within would gradually be smothered to death. Sundar's fate was to be just as unpleasant. He was beaten, stripped of his clothes and then violently thrown down a dry well, topped by a heavy iron lid. By his own account, the floor of the well was carpeted with the human bones and putrid flesh of previous victims.

It was only a question of time before either Sundar Singh would be suffocated by the terrible stench of death or he would die from starvation. One thing, however, sustained him. When he had first seen his vision of Christ, he reported experiencing a strong sense of peace and joy. This feeling, he claimed, remained with him always, even at times of distress and persecution. The effect of the vision – which, he maintained, was objective and entirely different from many other mystical experiences he was to have later on – was permanent; and that feeling of peace and joy stayed

with him throughout the duration of his incarceration in the well.

Sundar passed the time in prayer until, on the third night, he heard a key grating in the lock above and the rattle of the withdrawn cover. He claimed that a voice now called to him to seize the rope that was lowered. His arm had been injured during the beating he had received, but fortunately there was a loop in the rope into which he placed his foot. He was then hauled up the well and was free. He claimed he then heard the lid being replaced and relocked. Once he was out in the fresh air, the pain in his injured arm simply disappeared and he is said to have rested until morning, then returning to the local caravanserai, an inn where groups of travellers would seek refreshment. He remained there for a short while before resuming preaching.

The reappearance of a man thought to be dead and safely entombed caused a furore. Sundar was arrested, brought before the head Lama and ordered to describe how his escape had taken place. His explanation of what had happened only enraged the Lama, however, who declared that someone must have stolen the key. But when he found it was still on his girdle, which never left him, he was said to have been terrified. The Lama, apparently cowed by the possibility that the escape was indeed a product of some kind of divine intervention, ordered Sundar to leave immediately and to go as far from the city as possible.

This, then, was the miracle in Tibet, when Sundar Singh was supposedly plucked from certain slow death. But was the hand that saved him divine or human? Certainly, Sundar's account has its weaknesses. How was it that, after his release, he was able to make it all the way back to the caravanserai without anyone commenting on his nakedness? In fact, such a sight was not as unusual in

The three lamas, above, posing in front of a pilgrimage shrine, are shown carrying traditional ritual objects – prayer wheels and rosaries. Buddhism, as practised in Tibet, is an amalgam of the Buddhism of India and indigenous religious beliefs.

Tibet as it would have been in Britain, say. There is, however, no getting away from the fact that someone could have stolen the key in order to secure Sundar's release, subsequently replacing it in the Lama's girdle, or there may have been a duplicate. Anyone who had been locked up for three days in the conditions he had to endure would, undoubtedly, feel confused and disorientated when eventually released. Perhaps this explains why he was unaware of any human presence when he finally gained his freedom. Another point to ponder is how, given the conditions of Sundar's entombment, he could have known he had been there for three days – although, of course, someone may have told him of this fact later.

A sceptic would have strong grounds, too, for pointing out that the tale rests on the unsupported witness of a single man. That man, besides being subject to a constant stream of mystical visions, had experienced many other wonders. He claimed to have made contact with a secret Indian Christian brotherhood whom he urged to declare themselves publicly; and to have met a *rishi* (hermit) of great age, the Maharishi of Kailash, in the Himalayas, who dwelt in a cave 13,000 feet (4,000 metres) above sea-level and imparted to him a series of apocalyptic visions. These, however, were never recorded; and the secret Christian brotherhood never declared themselves. Then again, the sceptic could also argue that, for all his concern with Christian truth, the *sadhu* was perhaps a bit of a romancer, given to flights of fantasy.

Of course, the sceptic should be left to believe what he wants to believe. But miracle or no miracle, the event cannot overshadow the fact that Sundar was a genuinely good man who, in his own lifetime, was revered by many as a saint.

HEAVENLY FORCES?

In fact, Sundar himself always tried to play down his psychic and mystical experiences, as well as his possession of a gift of healing. He found that a reputation for miracle-mongering pandered to the public's taste for the bizarre and that he thereby risked diverting attention to himself and away from Christ. His own view of the affair in Tibet was that it had been heavenly forces at work. However, he would probably have been the last person to have wanted to make a production out of the so-called miracle. Glorification of himself, or even the name of the God he served, was entirely foreign to him.

By the 1920s, Sadhu Sundar Singh had become something of a household name. He made many trips, financed by friends, to Ceylon, Burma, Malaysia, China, Japan, America, Australia and Europe. He preached wherever he went and met with many prominent churchmen, among whom he was to gain a high reputation. Through these trips, he also made a deep impression on thousands of ordinary people of many races. But there were just a few who regarded him with suspicion and branded him a confidence trickster who told lies to support a cause in which he had come to believe. He continued to visit Tibet, and the country that had been the source of his deepest revelation also turned out to be the place where he met his end. Sundar Singh finally disappeared, without trace, somewhere in the Himalayas, in 1929.

ARIGO:SURGEON EXTRAORDINARY

HE OPERATED ON THE DYING WITH ONLY A RUSTY KNIFE – AND APPARENTLY CURED THEM. WAS THIS HUMBLE BRAZILIAN, WHO PERFORMED MANY SUCH SURGICAL MIRACLES, WORKING 'UNDER SPIRIT GUIDANCE'?

A priest had arrived to administer to the dying woman. Candles were lit, and relatives and friends were gathered around her bedside in the town of Congonhas do Campo, Brazil. Her death, from cancer of the uterus, was expected at any moment.

Suddenly, one of those present rushed from the room, returning moments later with a large knife from the kitchen. He ordered everyone to stand back. Then, without warning, he pulled the sheets from the woman and plunged the kitchen knife into her vagina.

After several brutal twists of the blade, he removed the knife and inserted his hand into the woman, withdrawing a huge tumour, the size of a grapefruit. He dropped the knife and the bloody tumour into the kitchen sink, sat down on a chair and began to sob.

Arigo is shown, below, performing a delicate eye operation in his back parlour. Although it was Arigo who went into a trance, the patient felt no pain – nor, it seems, any fear – despite the unhygienic surroundings, primitive lighting and complete lack of anaesthetics.

A relative rushed off to fetch a doctor; and the rest stood silently as if transfixed by the astonishing scene just witnessed. The patient was unperturbed: she had felt no pain at all during the 'operation', and what is more, the doctor confirmed that there was no haemorrhaging or other ill-effects. He also confirmed that the growth was a uterine tumour.

This extraordinary incident proved to be a turning point in the lives of the two people concerned. The woman recovered her health completely. And the man who had performed the 'surgery', José Arigo, suddenly found himself in great demand from people whose doctors had given them up as incurable. Yet he could not even remember 'operating' on the woman.

PSYCHIC SURGERY

Later, when such startling surgery became a daily occurrence in Congonhas do Campo – Arigo's home town – it was realised that he entered a trance state whenever he treated the sick. His patients also noticed he spoke with a German accent, allegedly because Dr Adolphus Fritz, who had died

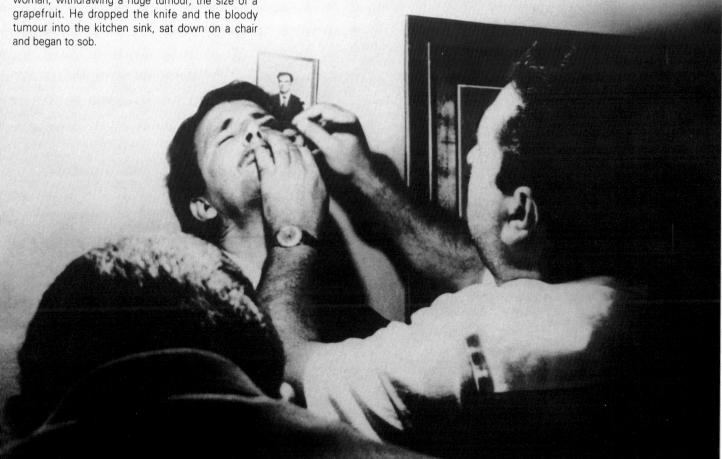

Puharich, a New York researcher with a keen interest in the paranormal who, after an initial visit, went back to Brazil with a team of doctors to investigate and film the phenomenon.

Puharich described the scene that first greeted him as 'a nightmare'. He wrote:

'These people step up – they're all sick. One had a big goitre. Arigo just picked up the paring knife, cut it open, popped the goitre out, slapped it in her hand, wiped the opening with a piece of dirty cotton, and off she went. It hardly bled at all.'

Puharich was also able to experience Arigo's extraordinary surgery for himself. He asked the Brazilian psychic surgeon to remove a small benign tumour from his arm. Arigo did so in seconds; and Dr Puharich was able to take the growth, and a film record of the surgery, back to the US for analysis.

In all the years that Arigo treated the sick by psychic surgery, there was never a single allegation that his unconventional treatment caused anyone any harm. Nevertheless, what he was doing was frowned upon by the authorities because Arigo had no medical qualifications. Eventually, in 1956, he was charged with practising illegal medicine.

Many people were willing to testify that Arigo had cured them of serious illnesses, but their testimonies only gave ammunition to the prosecution case. Arigo was given a prison sentence, which was reduced to eight months on appeal, and was fined. But just before he was put into prison, the Brazilian president, Kubitschek, gave him a pardon.

Then eight years later, he was charged again. Kubitschek was no longer president and Arigo was jailed for 16 months this time. After seven months, he was freed, pending an appeal, but eventually had to serve a further two months in prison, in 1965. During both periods, however, the warden allowed him out of his cell both to visit the sick and to operate on them.

ARIGO INVESTIGATED

The man who had to hear that appeal was Judge Filippe Immesi, a Roman Catholic with little knowledge of Arigo. But the more he studied the case, the more difficult it became for him to make a decision without seeing the astonishing psychic surgery for himself.

One day, unannounced, he visited Congonhas do Campos with a friend, who was a district attorney from another part of Brazil. Despite their anonymity, Arigo recognised them immediately as representatives of the law and invited them to see the 'operations' from close quarters. He knew that he was breaking the law, but thought the authorities might as well satisfy themselves that fraud was not taking place.

A near-blind woman with cataracts was one of the first patients they saw being treated, and Arigo asked the judge to hold her head. Though he felt queasy, he agreed to do so. John G. Fuller, author of *Arigo: Surgeon of the Rusty Knife*, quotes this testimony from Judge Immesi:

'I saw him pick up what looked like a pair of nail scissors. He wiped them on his sport shirt, and used no disinfectant of any kind. Then I saw him cut straight into the cornea of the patient's eye. She did not blench, although she was fully conscious. The cataract was out in a matter of seconds. The

in 1918, was said still to be 'operating' directly through him.

On most days when Arigo's clinic opened at 7 a.m., there was already a queue of some 200 people waiting. Some he would treat in a rapid and often brutal fashion, pushing them against a wall, jabbing an unsterilised knife into them, then wiping it clean on his shirt. Yet they felt no pain or fear. There was very little blood, and the wound would knit together immediately, healing in days.

Not everyone received psychic surgery, however. In some instances, he would simply glance at patients, diagnose their problems without asking any questions, and then write a prescription rapidly. The medicines prescribed were usually well-known drugs made by leading companies, but in large doses and combinations that were surprising according to conventional medical knowledge. Yet they cured people.

One conservative estimate suggests that he treated half-a-million patients in a five-year period. These included people from all walks of life: rich and poor alike, it made no difference to Arigo because he never accepted money or gifts for his services.

During the 1950s and 1960s, Arigo became something of a national hero in Brazil and hardly a day passed without newspapers headlining his latest healing miracles. Patients came from all over the world. He also attracted the attention of Andrija

José Arigo is seen, above, in jail. During two periods of imprisonment for practising medicine illegally, his jailers secretly let him out to perform operations on the sick, as successfully as ever.

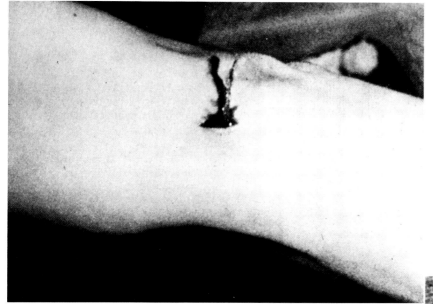

whose body was riddled with cancer. She and her husband were friends of Dr José Hortencia de Madeiros, an X-ray specialist with the State Institute of Cardiology, who took a close interest in the case. The cancer was discovered when she was rushed to a Sao Paulo clinic with symptoms of intestinal obstruction. It found that a tumour was blocking the transverse colon, and a colostomy was performed.

Later she entered the Central Cancer Hospital in the same city for another operation, where it was found that the cancer had spread dramatically. Her weight had dropped by nearly half, and the surgeon reported that she was totally beyond the resources of medical science.

So, as a last resort, she was taken to Arigo. Dr Madeiros accompanied the couple on the long trip to Congonhas do Campos, where the dying woman had to be carried into the clinic. Being an Austrian,

district attorney and I were speechless, amazed. Then Arigo said some kind of prayer as he held a piece of cotton in his hand. A few drops of liquid suddenly appeared on the cotton and he wiped the woman's eye with it. We saw this at close range. She was cured.'

What Judge Immesi saw convinced him that Arigo was a remarkable man who deserved to be the subject of scientific study. But the law was beyond doubt. What Arigo was doing was illegal and he would have to be punished – even though he was helping people. However, the judge looked for every possible excuse to reduce the sentence, with the result that Arigo was sent back to prison for just two months. While he was serving that sentence, Arigo's case was under review by the Federal Supreme Court, and it eventually decided to drop the charges against him. He was released on 8 November 1965.

MEDICAL TESTIMONY

The judge, of course, was not a medical man but he gave special attention to doctors' testimonies before reaching a verdict. There were several who had experience of Arigo's 'operations' and who were also prepared to say so in public. One of these was Dr Ary Lex, a distinguished Brazilian surgeon, a specialist in surgery of the stomach and digestive systems, lecturer at the Surgical Clinic of Sao Paulo University, and author of a standard textbook for Brazilian medical students.

Like Judge Immesi, Dr Lex was invited to hold a patient's head in his hands while Arigo operated. He witnessed four operations in half-an-hour and was satisfied that what Arigo was doing was paranormal. But he was not so impressed with the prescriptions. 'They were absolutely ridiculous,' he told author and psychic researcher, Guy Playfair. 'Some of them were obsolete medicines which were only still being made because he prescribed them.' A number of them, he said, were also dangerous in the doses prescribed, and expensive.

But however absurd the prescriptions may have seemed, their effects were frequently startling. One such case concerned a young Polish woman

Andrija Puharich, investigator of the paranormal, paid Arigo a visit to see the 'psychic surgeon' in action. He asked Arigo to remove the benign tumour from his arm and Arigo immediately made a deep incision (top) and then cut out the tumour with his unsterilised penknife, above.

the husband spoke to 'Dr Fritz' in German and he replied in that language. Then Arigo glanced at the sick woman, scribbled a prescription, and said: 'You take this, and get well'.

Dr Madeiros administered the abnormal dosage of drugs prescribed and the patient showed signs of improvement within a week. After six weeks, her weight had returned to normal. She then visited Arigo again, who announced that she was out of danger and gave her two more prescriptions. On a third visit to the psychic surgeon, the patient was told that she was completely healed and he advised her to 'undo the operation' – a reference to the colostomy that enabled the body's waste to be passed through the abdomen into a bag. Arrangements were made for the operation to be reversed; and when her abdomen was opened, the surgeons confirmed that all signs of cancer had vanished.

Arigo was killed in a car crash in January, 1971, having told several people that he would not see them again. The techniques he used to cure the sick remain a mystery. Arigo himself offered no explanation, except to give credit to Jesus and Dr Fritz. Once, when he saw a film of himself performing operations, he had fainted.

A PERILOUS MEDIUM

THE BRAZILIAN PSYCHIC CARMINE MIRABELLI HAD AN EXTRAORDINARY RANGE OF PARANORMAL SKILLS THAT WERE OFTEN AN EMBARRASSMENT TO HIS FAMILY AND COLLEAGUES

One day in 1911, a young man who was working as an assistant in a shoe shop in São Paulo, Brazil, was dismissed from his job. Apparently, his employer objected to the fact that shoe boxes kept flying off the shelves when the young man was near by. The dismissed employee, whose name was Carmine Mirabelli, afterwards spent 19 days in an asylum under the observation of two unusually sympathetic doctors. One of these, Dr Felipe Ache, declared that, while the young man was not normal, he was not sick, either. He concluded that his psychic abilities were 'the result of the radiation of nervous forces that we all have, but that [he] has in extraordinary excess'.

Dr Ache's colleague, Dr Franco da Rocha, described how Mirabelli was able to make a skull rotate on top of a glass without the need for touch – just by looking at it. 'Nor was that all,' the doctor added. 'When I picked up the skull, I felt something strange in my hands, something fluid, as if a globular liquid were touching my palm. When I concentrated my attention further, I saw something similar to an irradiation pass over the skull, as when you rapidly expose a mirror to luminous rays.'

This was the beginning of the remarkable career of the Brazilian medium Carmine Mirabelli, who was born in 1889, the son of a Protestant pastor of Italian origin. Credited with the ability to produce every known phenomenon of a medium's repertoire, he was possibly the greatest medium of all time. In addition to regular demonstrations of telepathy, clairvoyance and precognition, his reported feats included automatic writing in more than 30 languages, and producing paintings and drawings in various styles. Although he was musically untrained, he could, while in a state of trance, sing and play the piano with skill. He was also able to paint or write at the same time that he was singing, and write a message in one language while conversing in another.

In addition to all this, he was a focus for poltergeist activity for a period of some 40 years. In his presence, both in and out of doors, objects would move around, appear out of thin air, catch fire or vanish with such regularity that members of his family came to regard such happenings as routine. He was also said to have the skill of levitation, and to be able to produce visible materialisations of the dead.

Not only did Mirabelli have extraordinary mediumistic gifts, he also had a tremendous zest for normal life. Someone who knew him well for 20 years – his biographer Eurico de Goes – describes him as a man of great energy and charisma, who was excitable, impulsive and impatient, yet tolerant and good natured. He was quite capable of buying as many as 10 suits at a time and giving most of them away. Nevertheless, he showed a considerable

Carmine Mirabelli, **right,** *had psychic powers that were first discovered in 1911. In addition to clairvoyance, psychokinesis and automatic writing, he was said to be able to levitate, and to produce materialisations of the dead. His most celebrated demonstration of levitation took place during a seance in São Paulo, at which his son Luiz was present. The medium rose slowly into the air and remained there long enough for the photograph,* **left.**

business acumen, and was always able to earn a good living by 'normal' means. Mirabelli embraced the Spiritist cause, and founded and directed centres in several towns in Brazil. But he was unpopular with orthodox Spiritists because of his tendency towards exhibitionism, his fondness for physical demonstrations, and the fact that he sometimes charged money for his services. But even one of his most severe critics, the Spiritist historian Carlos Imbassahy, had to admit that there was no doubt that his mediumship was genuine.

In his book *O Espiritismo a Luz Dos Fatos* ('Spiritism in the Light of the Facts'), which was published in 1952, Imbassahy relates an incident when Mirabelli was brought, uninvited, to his house. 'There was nobody I less wanted to see,' Imbassahy wrote; for he feared 'this perilous mediumship' would start smashing his crockery.

Instead, the 'perilous medium' embarked on a detailed account of the life of one of Imbassahy's friends (whom Mirabelli had never met). Then a servant brought in some bottles of water and put them on a table some 16 feet (5 metres) from where Mirabelli was sitting. 'Immediately,' said Imbassahy, 'in full view of us all, one of the bottles rose halfway up the height of the others and hit them with full force for five or ten seconds, before returning to its place... This was seen and heard clearly, with no shadow of hesitation.'

Meanwhile, both the medium's hands were being held. Imbassahy would have been only too happy to denounce Mirabelli as a fraud, but he was honest enough to state that he was left 'with the unshakeable certainty' of his abilities.

Eurico de Goes' biography of Mirabelli is crammed from start to finish with detailed accounts of an enormous variety of phenomena, some of them quite extraordinary. At one seance, for instance, the handcuffed medium rose into the air and dematerialised. The handcuffs fell to the floor.

▟▟ THE PHENOMENA OF

MATERIALISATION WERE

ASTOUNDING. THE FIGURES WERE

NOT ONLY COMPLETE, THEY WERE NOT

ONLY PHOTOGRAPHED, BUT MEDICAL

MEN MADE MINUTE EXAMINATIONS

WHICH LASTED SOMETIMES AS LONG

AS FOR FIFTEEN MINUTES AND

STATED THAT THE NEWLY

CONSTITUTED HUMAN BEINGS HAD

PERFECT ANATOMICAL STRUCTURE. **▟▟**

NANDOR FODOR, ENCYCLOPEDIA OF

PSYCHIC SCIENCE

The seance room where the levitation took place is shown **right.** *The room was recognised as being the one in the levitation photograph when a team of psychical researchers visited the house in 1973. The essential clues were the mouldings round the light fitting in the ceiling, the two doors (partly hidden here by the dividing screen) and the fact that light coming through the window would have cast a shadow similar to the one in the levitation picture. Since the room is about 16 feet (5 metres) high, it is estimated that Mirabelli rose to about 8 feet (2.5 metres) from the ground.*

Mirabelli was eventually found, lying down and chanting in Latin, in a nearby locked room.

On another occasion, when Eurico de Goes was on his way to visit Mirabelli, he remembered he had left his umbrella at home. As he entered Mirabelli's house, his umbrella promptly fell from the ceiling. Apparent teleportation was also witnessed by the British poet-diplomat Sir Douglas Ainslie, who arrived at a private house in São Paulo and found his travelling clock on the hall table. He had last seen it inside a suitcase in his hotel room.

EXPRESS JOURNEY

In another incident related by Eurico de Goes, Mirabelli was waiting for a train with a group of friends when they suddenly noticed he was nowhere to be seen. His worried friends telephoned to the house they were heading for, in a town 50 miles (80 kilometres) away. They were told the medium was already there.

In 1973, the Brazilian Institute for Psychobiophysical Research (IBPP) appointed a team of investigators to compile a file on Mirabelli. The team was headed by the leading Brazilian parapsychologist Hernani G. Andrade. In a few weeks, the file was bulging with firsthand testimony. They managed to locate and interview three of the medium's sons, none of whom claimed to have inherited any of his father's paranormal skills. Cesar Augusto Mirabelli was a police investigator with São Paulo's flying squad. He was highly critical of the Spiritist movement, 99 per cent of which, in his opinion, was 'deceit, mystification or bad faith'. He added: 'If my father were a fraud, I would certainly say so.' However, Cesar insisted, fraud was out of the question; and phenomena were often produced just for the family. Among several examples he described was the following: 'We had an ornamental porcelain vase, about 60 centimetres [2 feet] high, weighing, I suppose, three to four kilos [about 7 pounds], standing on a kind of tripod... Suddenly, Father started to look at the corner where the vase was, and I started to look as well. The vase just rose into the air about 40 centimetres [16 inches]. Then, all at once, it turned, picked up speed and smashed itself to pieces against a wall, 2 metres [6 feet] away.' This kind of thing, Cesar said, would happen 'almost every day, any time and at any place'.

BURIED ALIVE

Regene Mirabelli, a businessman and amateur hypnotist, also had plenty of memories of an unusual home life. Once, on hearing an extraordinary noise, he rushed into the living room to find his mother buried beneath a pile of all the furniture. His mother was, he said, resigned to this sort of thing. Indeed, it was not unusual for her to spend half an hour laying the table, only to find, the moment her back was turned, the whole setting swept to the floor.

Mirabelli's eldest son, Luiz, had become a successful hardware salesman. He remembered a car journey in the open country during which the driver was suddenly slapped violently in the face by an invisible assailant. Mirabelli then told him to engage first gear, 'because "they" are trying to push us backwards'. Whereupon, said Luiz, the car – in first gear – did indeed start to move in reverse.

This remarkable series of pictures shows Mirabelli apparently controlling the gradual materialisation of a complete human form. The entity's robe and hair suggest an African or Indian origin for the materialisation.

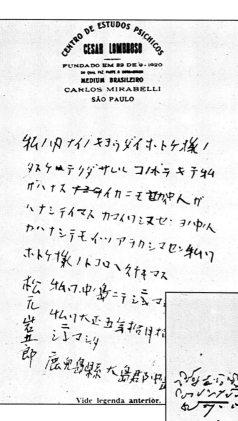

Vide legenda anterior.

One of Mirabelli's most uncanny gifts was the ability, when in a state of trance, to write automatic messages in over 30 languages. These examples include a message in Japanese, left, supposedly from one Iwagoro Matsumoto, who died on 10 October 1916; a message supposedly in Arabic, below, written in 12 minutes on 22 October 1924; and another that seems to be in Hebrew, bottom.

Vide legenda anterior.

Carmine Mirabelli — o maior medium de todos os tempos tanto de efeitos físicos como de efeitos intelectuais. As fotografias de materialização, ou os fac-similes de psicografia, comprovam a grande e inimitável capacidade metérgica de Mirabelli. Aliás na parte psicográfica, extensa e variada, e de um xenoglossismo simplesmente assombroso, se vêem communicações, escritas em rápidos minutos, muitas com mais de 10 folhas de papel almaço, em espanhol, italiano, latim, holandês, checo, alemão, japonês, russo, turco, hebraico, albanês, chinês, grego (moderno e antigo) e outros idiomas, alguns até com os seus dialetos. Damos a seguir uns fac-similes psicográficos.

Luiz was also present at one of the most celebrated incidents in his father's life. It happened during a seance in a well-lit room. Mirabelli rose slowly into the air, stayed there long enough for a photograph to be taken, and then descended to the ground slowly. But Luiz described the incident as if it were nothing especially remarkable .

During the IBPP investigation, the team met a São Paulo estate agent named Fenelon Alves Feitosa, who had known the medium well, and still held weekly Spiritist meetings in his memory. As it happened, Senhor Feitosa had just been asked to sell a house that he recognised as being one of Mirabelli's former centres.

The team went to visit the house, at 6 Rua Natal, in the Tucuruvi district. As they were going through the rooms, they recognised one of them as the scene of the levitation photograph. It seemed that the light coming through the window would have cast a shadow similar to the one seen in the photograph. The room was about 16 feet (5 metres) high and, in the photograph, Mirabelli's feet appear to be at least half that distance from the floor.

MOVING EXPLANATION

In December 1935, the Journal of the Society for Psychical Research (SPR) in London carried a long report on Mirabelli by Theodore Besterman that added to the controversy surrounding the medium. Besterman had witnessed a number of incidents involving the movement of objects, but remained sceptical. He asserted that 'hidden threads' were the explanation, although he admitted that he had never found any. He had watched a piece of board revolving on top of a bottle – which puzzled him – and had also witnessed Mirabelli writing more than 1,700 words in 53 minutes in French, a language that he is thought not to have learned.

'Mirabelli left me in no doubt that he was purely and simply fraudulent,' Besterman said in 1973. 'Once I had expressed this opinion, none of his followers would talk to me.'

Fortunately, other investigators were not so tactless. The eminent embryologist Hans Driesch, who was also a president of the SPR, witnessed at least one 'most impressive' demonstration of psychokinesis in 1928. And in 1934, May C. Walker of the American SPR described 'the most impressive telekinesis I have ever seen' after a session in which, among other things, a fan began to 'wriggle about, as if alive' in her hand.

One of the few Brazilians to make a systematic test of Mirabelli's skills was a well-known doctor and public health official, Dr Thadeu de Medeiros. The medium worked for a time in the doctor's clinic as a paranormal diagnostician. But bottles of medicine kept flying around the room, so this phase of his career also came to an abrupt end.

In 1960, Dr E. J. Dingwall of the SPR lamented that the Mirabelli case 'remains another of those unsolved mysteries with which the history of parapsychology abounds'. He put much of the blame on Besterman, for not keeping proper records.

Mirabelli died in 1951. His son Cesar has movingly described how, while they were on the way to the local cinema, the medium dashed across the road to buy his son an ice cream. He was hit by a car, and died without regaining consciousness.

HEALING THROUGH HORROR

DEVOTEES OF A DECEASED DEACON OF PARIS UNDERWENT TORTURES THAT SHOULD HAVE BEEN MORE THAN FLESH COULD BEAR. YET THEY SURVIVED, AND WERE OFTEN HEALED

The strange events that took place in the little Paris churchyard of St Médard between 1727 and 1732 sound so incredible, and so preposterous, that the modern reader is tempted to dismiss them as pure invention. However, this would be a mistake, for an impressive mass of documents – including accounts by doctors, magistrates and other respectable public figures – attests to their genuineness. The miracles undoubtedly took place. But no doctor, philosopher or scientist

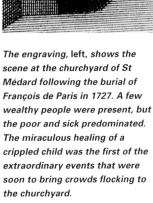

The engraving, left, shows the scene at the churchyard of St Médard following the burial of François de Paris in 1727. A few wealthy people were present, but the poor and sick predominated. The miraculous healing of a crippled child was the first of the extraordinary events that were soon to bring crowds flocking to the churchyard.

François de Paris, Deacon of Paris, left, *gained the love of the poor and the enmity of the Church hierarchy during his short life. Uniquely among clerics of the time, he worked with his own hands. Here, he is seen weaving a tapestry; the proceeds of its sale were to go to the poor.*

The prodigious feats performed by the devotees of François de Paris, as shown right, *were all repulsive in some way. Women were beaten with clubs, pounded with rocks, and stabbed with spears and swords. Others plunged their heads into fire or licked the ulcers of the sick. Yet they emerged from their ordeals unharmed.*

During his life, de Paris practised cruel self-mortifications. In the course of his devotions, he would whip himself with barbed flails, as in the illustration above. *In a similar way, the miraculous activities of his devotees seemed to show that God could enable human beings to endure any torture – and even transform it into pleasure for the victim.*

has even begun to explain how they could possibly have come about.

They began with the burial of François de Paris, the Deacon of Paris, in May 1727. François was only 37 years old, yet he was already widely revered as a holy man, with powers of healing. He was a follower of Bishop Cornelius Jansen, who taught that men can be saved only by divine grace, not by their own efforts. The Deacon had no doubt whatever that his own healing powers came from God.

INSTANT CURE

Great crowds followed his coffin, many weeping. It was laid in a tomb behind the high altar of St Médard. Then the congregation filed past, laying their flowers on the corpse. A father supported his son, a cripple, as he leaned over the coffin. Suddenly, the child went into convulsions; he seemed to be having a fit. Several people helped to drag him, writhing, to a quiet corner of the church. Suddenly, the convulsions stopped. The boy opened his eyes, looked around in bewilderment, and then slowly stood up. A look of incredulous joy crossed his face; then, to the astonishment of the spectators, he began to dance up and down, singing and laughing. His father found it impossible to believe, for the boy was using his withered right leg, which had virtually no muscles. Later, it was claimed that this leg had become as strong and normal as the other.

The news spread. Within hours, cripples, lepers, hunchbacks and blind men were rushing to the church. At first, few 'respectable' people believed the stories of these miraculous cures – the majority of the Deacon's followers were poor folk. The rich preferred to leave their spiritual affairs in the hands of the Jesuits, who were more cultivated and worldly. But it soon became clear that ignorance and credulity could not be used as a blanket explanation for all stories of such marvels. Deformed

limbs, it was said, were being straightened; hideous growths and cancers were disappearing without trace; and horrible sores and wounds were healing instantly.

The Jesuits declared that the miracles were either a fraud or the work of the Devil: the result was that most of the better-off in Paris flatly refused to believe that anything unusual was taking place in the churchyard of St Médard. But a few men of intellect were drawn by curiosity, and they invariably returned from the churchyard profoundly shaken. Sometimes, they recorded their testimony in print: some, such as Philippe Hecquet, attempted to explain the events by natural causes. Others, such as the Benedictine Bernard Louis de la Taste, attacked those who performed the miracles on theological grounds, but were unable to expose any deception by them, or any error on the part of the witnesses. Indeed, the accumulation of written testimony was such that David Hume, one of the greatest of philosophers, wrote in *An Enquiry Concerning Human Understanding*:

'There surely never was a greater number of miracles ascribed to one person... But what is more extraordinary; many of the miracles were immediately proved upon the spot, before judges of unquestioned integrity, attested by witnesses of credit and distinction, in a learned age... Where shall we find such a number of circumstances, agreeing to the corroboration of one fact?'

One of those who investigated the happenings was a lawyer, Louis Adrien de Paige. When he told his friend, the magistrate Louis-Basile Carré de Montgeron, what he had seen, the magistrate assured him, patronisingly, that he had been taken in by conjuring tricks – the kind of 'miracles' performed by tricksters at fairgrounds. But he finally agreed to go with de Paige to the churchyard, if only for the pleasure of pointing out how the lawyer

Marie Anne Couronneau, left, was completely paralysed in her left leg. Two doctors pronounced the affliction 'absolutely incurable'. But she was allegedly healed by the convulsionnaires of St Médard – and celebrated by running up a flight of stairs and waving her crutches in the air.

The principal chronicler of the miracles of St Médard, Louis-Basile de Montgeron, presented the first volume of his account to King Louis XV, as shown below left – and was thrown into prison for his pains. The royal displeasure, prompted by the Jesuits' disapproval of de Paris and all his works, was eventually visited on the convulsionnaires: they, and many of their supporters, were dragged off to the Bastille, below.

had been deceived. They went there on the morning of 7 September 1731. De Montgeron left the churchyard a changed man – and even endured prison rather than deny what he had seen that day.

EXTRAORDINARY SPECTACLE

The first thing the magistrate saw when he entered the churchyard was a number of women writhing on the ground, twisting themselves into the most startling shapes, sometimes bending backwards until the backs of their heads touched their heels. These ladies were all wearing a long cloth undergarment that fastened around the ankles. De Paige explained that this was now obligatory for all women who wished to avail themselves of the Deacon's miraculous powers. In the early days, when women had stood on their heads or bent their bodies convulsively, prurient young men had begun to frequent the churchyard to view the spectacle.

However, in spite of this requirement, there was no lack of male devotees of the deceased Abbé to assist in the activities in the churchyard. De Montgeron was shocked to see that some of the women and girls were being sadistically beaten – at least, that is what at first appeared to be going on. Men were striking them with heavy pieces of wood and iron. Other women lay on the ground, apparently crushed under immensely heavy weights. One girl was naked to the waist: a man was gripping her nipples with a pair of iron tongs and twisting them violently. De Paige explained that none of these women felt any pain; on the contrary, many begged for more blows. And, most miraculous of all, an incredible number were cured of deformities or diseases by this violent treatment.

In another part of the churchyard, they saw an attractive, pink-cheeked girl of about 19, who was sitting at a trestle table and eating. That seemed normal enough, until de Montgeron looked more closely at the food on the plate, and realised from its appearance – as well as from the smell that reached him – that it was human excrement. In between mouthfuls of this sickening fare, she drank a yellow liquid which, de Paige explained, was urine. This girl had come to the churchyard to be cured of what we would now call a neurosis: she had to wash her hands hundreds of times a day, and was so fastidious about her food that she would taste nothing that had been touched by another human hand. The Deacon had indeed cured her. Within days, she was eating excrement and drinking urine, and did so with every sign of enjoyment. Such cases might not be remarkable in asylums; but what was more extraordinary – even preposterous – was that after one of these meals, she opened her mouth as if to be sick, and milk came pouring out. De Paige collected a cupful; it was, apparently, perfectly ordinary cow's milk.

" ONE GIRL WAS NAKED TO THE WAIST: A MAN WAS GRIPPING HER NIPPLES WITH A PAIR OF IRON TONGS AND TWISTING THEM VIOLENTLY. DE PAIGE EXPLAINED THAT NONE OF THESE WOMEN FELT ANY PAIN; ON THE CONTRARY, MANY BEGGED FOR MORE BLOWS. **"**

Long after the suppression of the activities at St Médard, bursts of religious zeal occasionally reappeared in Paris. One of the many crucifixions indulged in by a girl named Sister Françoise, for instance, was recorded by the scientist La Condamine. After more than three hours on the cross, *as below right, she was taken down, exhausted but little the worse for the ordeal.*

After staggering away from the eater of excrement, de Montgeron had to endure a worse ordeal. In another part of the churchyard, a number of women had volunteered to cleanse suppurating wounds and boils by sucking them clean. Trying hard to prevent himself vomiting, de Montgeron watched as someone unwound a dirty bandage from the leg of a small girl; the smell was horrible. The leg was a festering mass of sores, some so deep that bone was visible. The woman who had volunteered to clean it was one of the *convulsionnaires* – she had been miraculously cured and converted by her bodily contortions, and God had now chosen her to demonstrate how easily human beings' disgust can be overcome. Yet even she blenched as she saw and smelled the gangrenous leg. She cast her eyes up to heaven, prayed silently for a moment, then bent her head and began to lap, swallowing the septic matter. When she moved her face further down the child's leg, de Montgeron could see that the wound was now clean. De Paige assured him that the girl would almost certainly be cured when the treatment was complete.

What de Montgeron saw next finally shattered his resistance and convinced him that he was witnessing something of profound significance.

A 16-year-old girl named Gabrielle Moler had arrived, and the interest she excited made de Montgeron aware that, even among this crowd of miraculous freaks, she was a celebrity. She removed her cloak and lay on the ground, her skirt modestly round her ankles. Four men, each holding a pointed iron bar, stood over her. When the girl smiled at them, they lunged down at her, driving their rods into her stomach. De Montgeron had to be restrained from interfering as the rods went through the girl's dress and into her stomach. He

looked for signs of blood staining her dress. But none came, and the girl looked calm and serene. Next, the bars were jammed under her chin, forcing her head back. It seemed inevitable that they would penetrate through to her mouth; yet when the points were removed, the flesh was unbroken. The men took up sharp-edged shovels, placed them against a breast, and then pushed with all their might; but the girl went on smiling gently. The breast, trapped between shovels, should have been cut off but it seemed impervious to the assault. Then, the cutting edge of a shovel was placed against her throat, and the man wielding it did his best to cut off her head; but he did not seem able even to dent her neck.

Dazed, de Montgeron watched as the girl was beaten with a great iron truncheon that was shaped like a pestle. A stone weighing half-a-hundredweight (25 kilograms) was raised above her body and dropped repeatedly from a height of several feet. Finally, de Montgeron watched her kneel in front of a blazing fire, and plunge her head into it. He could feel the heat from where he stood; yet her hair and eyebrows were not even singed. When she picked up a blazing chunk of coal and proceeded to eat it, de Montgeron could stand no more and left.

Nevertheless, he went back repeatedly, until he had enough materials for the first volume of an amazing book. He presented it to the King, Louis XV, who was so shocked and indignant that he had de Montgeron thrown into prison. Yet de Montgeron felt he had to bear witness and was to publish two more volumes following his release, full of precise scientific testimony concerning the miracles.

MIND OVER MATTER

In the year following de Montgeron's imprisonment, 1732, the Paris authorities decided that the scandal was becoming unbearable and closed down the churchyard. But the *convulsionnaires* had discovered that they could perform their miracles anywhere, and continued for many years.

A hardened sceptic, the scientist La Condamine, was as startled as de Montgeron when, in 1759, he watched a girl named Sister Françoise crucified on a wooden cross, nailed by the hands and feet over a period of several hours, and stabbed in the side with a spear. He noticed that all this obviously hurt the girl, and that her wounds bled when the nails were removed; but she seemed none the worse for an ordeal that would have killed most people.

So how can we possibly explain these miracles from the standpoint of the late 20th century? Some writers believe they involved a kind of self-hypnosis. But while this could explain the excrement-eater and the woman who sucked festering wounds, it is less plausible in explaining Gabrielle Moler's feats of endurance. These remind us rather of descriptions of the practices of fakirs. For example, J.G. Bennett, in his autobiography *Witness*, describes watching a Dervish ritual in which a razor-sharp sword was placed across the belly of a naked man, after which two heavy men jumped up and down on it – all without even marking the flesh. What seems to be at work here is some form of 'mind over matter', far more effective than mere hypnosis, which is not yet understood but which certainly merits serious attention.

THE COSMIC ORGASM

WILHELM REICH BELIEVED THAT THE SECRET OF PHYSICAL AND MENTAL HEALTH IS CONTAINED IN THE ORGASM, AND THAT SEXUAL ENERGY IS TANGIBLE AND CAN BE HARNESSED TO RID THE WORLD OF ALL ILLS

Wilhelm Reich (1897-1957), **right,** *demonstarted bold theories about the importance of the orgasm in both individual and collective life. He believed that orgasm – and only heterosexual orgasm – could, if uninhibited enough, relieve men and women of all tensions and establish a total inner harmony. He even went further, claiming to have created 'bions', substances halfway between dead and living tissue, which could become living – albeit primitive – matter.*

T he quest to discover the secret of life, and to identify some force that distinguishes living protoplasm from inanimate matter, has obsessed occultists, alchemists and scientists alike for centuries. Although, in most cases, the investigator has pursued knowledge for its own sake, in others he has tried to usurp the divine prerogative and actually create life from inorganic material. Occasionally, he has even claimed to have succeeded in this.

As late as the 1930s, a London-based alchemist named Archibald Cockren, attempted to create life in the form of the 'alchemical tree': this was supposed to be a living mineral, described in the 16th century by Paracelsus as 'a wonderfull and pleasant shrub, which the Alchymists call their Golden hearb'. The poet C. R. Cammell said that he had seen this mineral 'hearb' in Cockren's laboratory and had watched it grow to a considerable size over a period of months.

But the claim to have created life has not been confined to eccentric occultists. The late Wilhelm Reich (1897-1957), a scientist with an impeccable academic background, asserted not only that he had created life but also that, by doing so, he had solved many mysteries of nature, from the causes of cancer to the significance of UFO sightings.

Reich was the son of prosperous Austrian-Jewish parents. After serving in the Austrian army during the First World War, he studied medicine at Vienna University and qualified as a doctor in 1922. While still a medical student, he studied the writings of Sigmund Freud (1856-1939) and other pioneer psychoanalysts, becoming convinced of the

P E R S P

A WASTE OF ENERGY?

Reich's highly controversial claims, such as having created life from inorganic matter – the alchemists' obsession, as illustrated *below* –

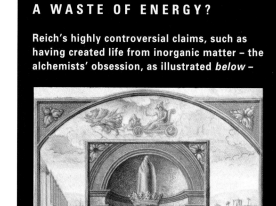

The hectic quest of the medieval alchemist for the secret of life – as depicted above, involved searching for an actual chemical or physical ingredient that could be isolated and used to create living tissue from dead or inorganic matter, Reich and his followers believed that he had succeeded in discovering radiating 'bions' – derived from sterilised sea sand – and that the radiations they gave off were the life-stuff of the Universe.

CTIVES

naturally gave his critics plenty of ammunition. An arch-sceptic of all matters paranormal, John Sladek certainly did not mince his words in the chapter on Reich in *The New Apocrypha*, particularly when describing Reich's 'disastrous ORANUR experiment'.

OR – Reichian shorthand for *'orgone radiation'* – was believed by his followers to be beneficial on a large scale. As his wife, Ilse Ollendorf Reich, explained: 'It was Reich's idea to help eradicate the terrible effects of the atom bomb through a three-fold attack: by using *orgone* energy to heal radiation sickness, to neutralize the effects of an atom bomb and . . . to immunize mankind against radiation'.

The ORANUR experiment consisted of exposing a large number of mice to radioactive material and then to beams of OR, which would, Reich and his research team were convinced, neutralize the harmful radioactivity. Very shortly, however, as Sladek describes, 'his assistants had noticed Geiger counters running wild, but of course they put it down to excesses of *orgone* energy. Forty test-animals died in one day, having all the symptoms of radiation poisoning. Then lab assistants began coming down with the same symptoms....' Reich's wife was similarly affected – so badly that she had to undergo surgery. But even so, Reich – with amazing obtuseness – consistently missed the point.

central importance of sexuality in human life. On 1 March 1919, he wrote in his diary: '. . . from my own experience, and from observation of myself and others, I have become convinced that sexuality is the centre around which revolves the whole of social life as well as the inner life of the individual'.

In 1920, Reich was accepted as a member of Freud's Vienna Psychoanalytical Society; and by 1922, as one of the co-founders of the Viennese Seminar for Psychoanalytic Therapy, he had become regarded by the elders of the analytical movement as an authority on therapeutic techniques.

But by 1927, Reich had begun to drift away from current Freudian orthodoxy. He was in fact developing a strand of early Freudian theory that Freud himself had neglected for over a quarter of a century: this concerned the *aktual* ('at the present time') neuroses.

In the formative period of psychoanalysis, Freud had classified neuroses into two groups: psychoneuroses that were caused by incidents that had happened long ago, particularly in early childhood; and *aktual* neuroses that were psychological illnesses, supposedly caused by current disturbances of healthy sexuality, such as premature ejaculation, or obsessive masturbation. Freud concentrated all his attention on the psychoneuroses and, after about 1900, scarcely ever mentioned the *aktual* neuroses.

▮▮SEXUAL EXCITATION, REICH REPORTED, WAS ACCOMPANIED BY A SIGNIFICANT INCREASE IN THE BIO-ELECTRICAL CHARGE OF THE GENITALS. ▮▮

Reich, however, concluded that Freud was mistaken, and that almost all illness, including schizophrenia and manic depression, resulted from the failure to achieve 'true orgasm', which he defined as 'the capacity for complete discharge of all dammed-up sexual excitation through involuntary pleasurable contractions of the body'. The object of psychoanalytical therapy, Reich argued, was to establish 'orgastic potency' and to enable the individual to achieve a sexual climax that would be long-lasting, fully satisfying and unaccompanied by fantasies or fetishes. It would also be without subsequent feelings of guilt or inadequacy; and above all, it would be the result of a heterosexual relationship.

Reich also believed that the failure of dammed-up sexual energy to find release in the convulsions of orgasm resulted in 'muscular armouring' – muscular tension and rigidity. This armouring reinforced the original disturbance, which in turn led to more tension and rigidity – a self-perpetuating process of physical and mental degeneration.

Neither the traditional Freudian type of analysis (the unveiling of repressed memories) nor Reich's own practice, based on examining 'present-day character', was adequate to cope with such armouring. For this, Reich developed a new technique, which involved character analysis, deep massage, breathing exercises and violent physical manipulation of the patient's body to break down tension and release blocked-up sexual energy. Reich called this process *vegetotherapy,* because he believed that the energies trapped by muscular armouring were stored in the vegetative (otherwise known as the autonomic, or involuntary) nervous system.

Reich was also interested in the nature of sexual energy. He believed it to be a specific force, comparable to the forces of gravitation and electromagnetism, and that it could be accumulated in the same way that electricity is stored in a battery. To prove his point, he embarked on a series of experiments to ascertain 'whether the sexual organs, in a state of excitation . . . show an increase in their bio-electric charge'. Volunteers were wired up and the results of their sexual activity monitored: the results were spectacular. Sexual excitation, Reich reported, was accompanied by a significant increase in the bio-electrical charge of the genitals; anxiety, pain and guilt, by a reduction. The orgasm was a biological thunderstorm.

In 1935, Reich (who was now living in Norway as a refugee from the Nazis) began an even more ambitious series of biological experiments. He subsequently announced to his astonished scientific contemporaries that he had succeeded in producing, from substances such as sterilised coal and soot, what he termed *'bions'.* These, he claimed, were energy vesicles (sacs), halfway between dead

The Orgone Energy Observatory at Orgonon near Rangeley, Maine, USA, is shown below. Reich and his supporters established this observatory in the hope that orgone energy could be detected and harnessed for the greater good of mankind. For a more detailed view of the effects of intensified orgone, the orgone energy accumulators, left, were used. Although quaintly resembling privies, they were believed to accumulate the orgone energy of anyone seated within. The energy thus collected and stored could, Reich believed, be used to treat virtually any kind of human ailment.

matter and living tissue, capable of developing into protozoa (single-cell organisms). One of Reich's assistants filmed these 'bions' through a microscope, but biologists were not impressed. The 'bions', they argued, were no more than tiny particles of non-living matter and their movements were the result of ordinary physical phenomena.

Undeterred by this criticism, Reich continued with his experiments. He concentrated his attention on a 'radiating *bion*' that he believed he had derived from sterilised sea sand; and, in 1939, he announced that the radiation given off by these sand-packet *bions* (which he named *'sapabions'*) was a hitherto unknown form of energy, the basic life-stuff of the Universe. He called it *'orgone'*, and devoted the rest of his life to studying it.

ORGONE ENERGY

In the same year that he claimed to have discovered *orgone* energy, Reich emigrated to the USA where he began to attract a small but enthusiastic following. He continued his research on *orgone*, which he maintained was identical with both the *vis animalis* ('animal force') of the ancient alchemists and the 'life force' – a mysterious quality distinguishing living from dead matter, as postulated by the philosopher Henri Bergson. *Orgone* was no metaphysical abstraction. It could not only be measured with an *'orgone* energy field meter' (a modified electroscope of Reich's own devising) but could be seen by the naked eye in 'the blue coloration of sexually excited frogs', and also collected and stored in an *'orgone* energy accumulator', another Reichian invention. These accumulators, said Reich, could be used in the treatment of every human ailment, from depression to cancer.

Orgone energy accumulators were (and are) boxes made of alternate layers of inorganic and organic material (usually metal and wood). The more layers there are, the more powerful the accumulator. Those intended for human use are large enough for the patient to sit inside; in appearance, they strongly resemble an old-fashioned privy.

As Reich grew older, his ideas about orgone *grew stranger. He published an increasing number of pamphlets on how to trap and utilise this mysterious but basic energy, derived from the accumulator, below, and also attracted bizarre followers, such as the American architect Frank Lloyd Wright, above, who defended his hero through Reich's last harrowing trial. Another of Reich's faithful, if somewhat flamboyant, disciples was the beat poet Allen Ginsberg, above right, seen tangling with the British police. Ginsberg adapted Reich's theories to advocate collecting* orgone *through the use of hard drugs and homosexual practices – something of which Reich would never have approved.*

Between 1939 and 1957, Reich published many articles and books, making increasingly astounding claims for *orgone*. Originally, he had regarded it as an energy exclusive to living organisms, but by 1951 he was asserting that it was the original building-matter of creation, the primal 'stuff' from which reality had evolved, and that physical matter was the offspring of the superimposition (the 'cosmic orgasm') of two streams of *orgone*. Everything from radio interference and the blueness of the sky (*orgone* was coloured blue) to hurricane formation and the force of gravity was a manifestation of *orgone*. The only exception was atomic radiation, which Reich saw as the antithesis of the life energy – a Satan to the Jehovah of *orgone*.

All this was strange enough, but even odder were Reich's writings on the subject of UFOs. Earth, Reich asserted, was the centre of an intergalactic conflict, and UFOs were the warships of the antagonists. One side was utterly evil, and extracted *orgone* from the Earth and its atmosphere with the intention of reducing the planet to a radioactive cinder; their opponents were allies of humanity and thus of Reich, and dedicated to replacing the stolen *orgone*.

Reich died in prison in 1957. He had been sentenced for defying a Federal injunction banning the sale of his accumulators on the grounds that they were fraudulent. For a time, it seemed that Reich and his theories would quickly be forgotten. Some of his followers became even odder than their teacher: one group, for instance, spent much time sitting in semi-darkness, clad in blue robes (in honour of *orgone),* attempting to communicate with their dead master through the ouija board. Other alleged Reichian groups, closely associated with the writers Allen Ginsberg and William Burroughs, combined Reichian theories with the advocacy of homosexuality and the use of psychedelic drugs, something that Reich would not himself have condoned.

However, some of Reich's writings have attracted more serious study, and a number of therapists, influenced by his ideas, now practise in major cities. But no one has yet attempted to repeat his laboratory work, with the object of establishing the extent to which his orgone experiments had any validity.

LIVE BURIAL

TO MOST PEOPLE, THE IDEA OF BEING BURIED ALIVE IS PURE NIGHTMARE. BUT SOME HAVE PERFECTED THE ART OF STAYING INTERRED FOR LONG PERIODS – FOR FAME AND FORTUNE OR, SO THEY SAY, TO GAIN ENLIGHTENMENT

During the mid-17th century, an astonishing incident occurred on the outskirts of Amritsar, in north-west India. Workmen, digging a ditch in a layer of brittle shale, found they had accidentally broken into a tomb. Inside, they found the dust-covered – and apparently mummified – body of a young yogi, sitting cross-legged and in faded orange robes. They decided to bring the body to the surface and, so the story goes, when the Sun's rays first touched the body's dry skin, it began to change. The yogi gradually stirred and, within a short time, was talking to the workmen, seemingly not much affected by the ordeal of having been buried alive. But he had an even greater

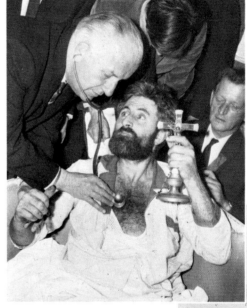

shock to impart to his saviours. His name was Ramaswami, he said, and he had descended voluntarily into his tomb about 100 years previously.

Within a month, news of the yogi's resurrection had spread far and wide in the subcontinent, and was taken by many Indians to be confirmation, if such were needed, of the reality of yogic powers. No one challenged Ramaswami, so universal was the belief in this feat. On the contrary, one famous historian, Arjun Singh, even journeyed to Amritsar to learn more of life in the previous century from one of its alleged former denizens. If Ramaswami was a charlatan, he was no ordinary one, because the historian came away impressed.

However, the story of Ramaswami, while providing a prototype for the phenomenon of live burial, is quite unsatisfactory as evidence. Further details are locked away in obscure publications in the Indian languages and are generally inaccessible to the Western researcher. In any event, should one discover a reference, it will almost certainly lack the kind of corroborative details that a

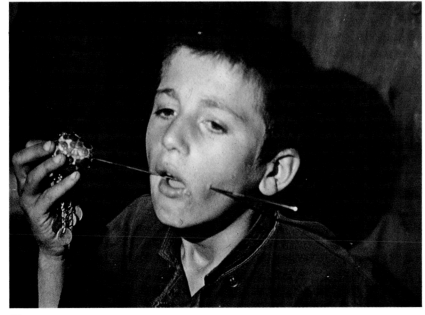

Westerner would find convincing, partly because these have always seemed incidental to the oriental mind, preoccupied as it has long been with philosophical or spiritual truths. More satisfactory from a Western standpoint are the records of a fakir called Haridas, who appeared in the Jammu region of India's north-west frontier in the late 1820s.

Haridas first came to prominence when Raja Dhyan Singh, a government minister, published a description of a four-month burial endured by Haridas that he himself witnessed. This was independently confirmed by at least one European doctor. When news of further triumphs reached the ears of the Maharaja of Lahore, an educated sceptic, he invited Haridas to his palace for a carefully controlled experiment. Several English doctors, as well as French and English military personnel, were invited along, the latter being asked to scrutinise the proceedings.

According to a lengthy account in the *Calcutta Medical Times*, the doctors immediately discovered that Haridas had cut away the muscles under his

The capacity of Indian yogis – or holy men – to endure even the most hideous self-inflicted pain without flinching – an ability showed by the young boy, bottom, far left – and to alter their metabolism at will has long been the stuff of travellers' tales. But the mystic East does not have the monopoly of mind over body. In 1968, Mike Meaney, an Irish barman from Kilburn, London, was buried in a wooden coffin for a record-breaking 61 days. As the coffin was lowered, he was in exuberant spirits left; and when he was exhumed, in front of an enormous crowd, below left, he was pronounced by the doctor, who examined him, far left, to be in excellent condition. Others aim to get above ground as fast as possible: in 1955, escapologist Derek Devero – watched over by a crowd, above – freed himself from his manacles and a mailbag, underground in Pollokshields, Glasgow, in just five minutes.

tongue, so that it could be doubled back to seal off the nasal passages at the back of the throat. For some days before his immurement, Haridas consumed only milk and yoghurt, and bathed in hot water. Finally, he fasted completely and, before all the witnesses, performed several extreme yogic ablutions to clean out his alimentary canal, including – we are told – swallowing a 30-yard (27-metre) strip of linen and regurgitating it. He closed his nose and ears with wax – a defensive measure against insects – and then settled into a cross-legged position, rolling his tongue back. The physicians found that, within seconds, his pulse was undetectable. 'He was physically dead,' declared one.

A 40-DAY ORDEAL

Haridas was wrapped in linen and placed in a large, padlocked chest, which was then sealed with the Maharaja's personal seal. The chest was buried and barley sown in the soil above it. Then a wall was built around the site, and guards were posted around the clock. Forty days later, the guests gathered again, this time to witness the fakir's unearthing. In the meantime, the barley had sprouted undisturbed, and the seal and locks had remained intact. Inside his shroud, Haridas was found in the same pose.

According to one of the witnesses, Sir Charles Wade, the fakir had all the appearance of a dead man – his legs and arms had shrunk and were rigid, his head lolled on one shoulder, and there was no detectable pulse in arm or temple. Haridas was massaged all over for minutes before signs of life returned. Doctors pulled back his tongue, unbunged his nose and ears, and inflated his lungs with bellows. He was back to normal within the hour. The Maharaja gave him a handful of diamonds; after that, he was lionised and showered with gifts wherever he went – for a while. For, despite performing several more times, without ever being proved a fraud, he was ignominiously drummed out of Indian high society for deflowering several of his female followers, and he was never heard of again.

About a year after Haridas' successful performance at Lahore, there was a report in the *Indian*

In the 1930s, the United States and Europe were treated to repeated demonstrations of live burials by three Egyptians – Tara Bey, Rahman Bey and Hamid Bey. While in England, Rahman Bey effected various 'mysterious' feats under the auspices of psychical researcher Harry Price, including live burial at Carshalton, Surrey, right. Although he emerged in good condition some time later, below right, his abilities were later shown to be only average tricks by Harry Houdini, who outdid everything the Beys performed.

The appropriately named Lucky, a tomcat, below, was found in a sealed drain in Bristol in June 1982. Workmen had blocked the drain five weeks before with Lucky in it. His only injury was a stiff neck. After a hearty meal, he was able to pose for the press with kennelmaid Joyce Alsworth.

Journal of Medical and Physical Science of a similar burial, by an unnamed fakir, at Jaisulmer. It might have been Haridas – for he, too, stopped the interior opening of the nostrils with his tongue and made similar yogic preparations. This fakir was sewn into a thick cloth bag and placed in a stone cell lined with brick, which in turn was sealed with stone slabs, bricked up and guarded night and day. At the end of a full month, he was removed from his tomb perfectly senseless: indeed, his skin was so dry and shrunken that he seemed to be almost mummified. His teeth were also jammed together so fast that an iron lever was needed to force them apart in order to administer a little water. Even so, he fully recovered in a few hours.

In the 1920s, three self-styled Egyptians – Tara Bey, Rahman Bey and Hamid Bey – aroused considerable interest during their tour of Europe and the USA. They performed live burials attended by newsmen and physicians, and in the ground of the witnesses' choosing. In what might be called the classic manner, they stopped their ears and noses with cotton, and consciously diminished their breathing and pulse rate. Tara Bey claimed this was achieved by willpower, together with pressure on certain nerve centres in the head and neck, and by retraction of the tongue to the back of the throat. Recovery was aided either by the attentions of his assistants or through something akin to post-hypnotic suggestion. But despite achieving apparently genuine burials for short periods – they were not in the same league as Haridas – they were accused at every turn of trickery.

HOUDINI TRIUMPHS AGAIN

Indeed, their tour ended in a double disgrace. To scotch rumours of fraud, Rahman Bey agreed to lie in a coffin in the Hudson River, but came up after only 19 minutes, just a few minutes longer than the world record for breath-holding. Magician Harry Houdini immediately saw his chance to expose the fakir as a fraud. Using his own not inconsiderable powers of breath-control, he spent all of one-and-a-half hours in a steel coffin at the bottom of a swimming pool at the Hotel Shelton, New York. Tara Bey, too, was trounced – by a Frenchman called Heuzé who was buried in an ordinary coffin for an hour. There was no need for mystical trances, he said, because – by keeping absolutely still and breathing slowly – there had been enough air.

It is easy enough to explain the burial feat by presupposing trickery, as openly advocated by the psychologist D. H. Rawcliffe in *Illustrated Magic* – or as implied in Ottaker Fischer's speculation, in the same work, that fakirs must have dug concealed tunnels leading to hollow trees, or used coffins with false bottoms or sliding panels.

The fact that most mendicant jugglers and magicians calling themselves fakirs have been revealed to be cunning tricksters has not helped matters either. In 1955, the pioneering ufologist John Keel, then aged about 25, was a syndicated journalist, drifting about India, and seeking out *jadoo wallahs* – performers of black magic and miracles. In his search for genuine mysteries, as recorded in his first book *Jadoo*, he saw very few and gradually became more cynical about their alleged accom-

plishments. But, even so, he had to admit some were genuine. So how are their feats achieved? If yoga is the means to the goal of *samadhi* – a super-conscious state of union with the totality of existence – then the Islamic fakir and his counterpart, the Hindu *sadhu*, differ from more philosophical or spiritual yogis by concentrating on the means and not the goal. Their aim is nothing less than mastery of their immediate existence by absolute control of their bodies, minds and psychic forces. This, they claim, can be accomplished only by years of gruelling discipline bordering on self-torture.

In *The Living Brain*, the neurologist Dr W. Grey Walter agreed that conscious control of autonomic processes would enable an adept to reduce his body 'to the state of an hibernating animal and can similarly be buried alive for days'. The comparison between the fakir's self-induced cataleptic state and animal hibernation was first proposed by James Braid, the physician who coined the term 'hypnosis', and the connection is clearly implied in the title of his *Observations on Trance, of Human Hibernation*, in which he discusses live burials. He concluded that yogis perfected their control through the use of self-hypnosis.

This association with animal hibernation is an obvious one, and has engendered a splendid piece of American folklore – that, from colonial times, pioneer folk in the hard mountain winters would systematically chill their old folk in freezing draughts, then pack them in snow until the spring thaw. However, laboratory studies – as cited by Andrija Puharich in *Physiological Psychology* – show that, although the yogi does indeed reduce his oxygen consumption and heartbeat, the two states are quite unalike. For example, Puharich claims that, in hibernation, the basal metabolic rate is low and in yogic trance it is high: in hibernation, blood sugar supply is much reduced, whereas in yogic trances it remains more or less the same or can even rise.

Thus, to this day, 'impossible' feats of suspended animation, as witnessed by many of integrity over the centuries, point to mind over matter but are as yet beyond scientific explanation.

An Indian fakir reclines, right, on a bed of sharp nails, his emaciated body showing signs of previous self-torture. It seems that anything – from sticking knives in oneself to firewalking – is possible while entranced. The vital bodily functions can also be slowed down until barely perceptible. It is under such conditions that yogis can remain underground for a considerable time.

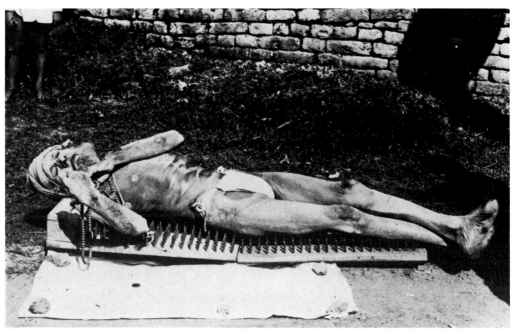

FEW PSYCHICS HAVE BEEN AS RENOWNED FOR THEIR WORLDLY ACHIEVEMENTS IN THE ARTS AND SCIENCES AS EMANUEL SWEDENBORG. HE BECAME INCREASINGLY FAMOUS FOR HIS ODD ABILITY TO LIVE IN BOTH THIS WORLD AND THE NEXT, TOO

O f the rare breed of encyclopedic intellects who excel in every branch of knowledge they study, surely the Swede Emanuel Swedenborg (1688-1772) was the strangest. He was, for example, a scientist highly skilled in anatomy, chemistry, mathematics and physics. He was also a psychologist and psychoanalyst, a theologian, a linguist fluent in nine languages, a competent craftsman in seven arts, and the inventor of at least 11 contrivances that lacked only 20th-century technology to perfect them. He was a metallurgist and mining engineer, and prolific author of works that were translated into 30 languages. And not only was he a gardener, musician and poet, he was also a psychic of high quality and the inspiration for a new Christian denomination.

SWEDENBORG – MAN OF UNACCOUNTABLE TALENTS

Swedenborg's career as a scientist, however, came to an abrupt end in 1745 when he received a vocational 'call' to become a theologian. As the former, he had been a pioneer – anticipating, for instance, by inductive methods, some of the findings of modern nuclear physics. His theories about the workings of the brain have been confirmed by modern technology. Yet, long before 1745, he had shown a marked interest in religious matters and had mystical experiences that were harbingers of his future course. Swedenborg did not consider himself eccentric in looking for the seat of the soul in the 'spiritous fluid' that he believed to be the essence of blood; and he seems always to have been aware of the existence of his guardian angel.

His first recorded psychical-spiritual experience occurred in 1736. A state of profound meditation led to a lengthy 'swoon' that he said 'cleared his brain', giving him great powers of mental penetration – a process that was to be repeated at least once in his lifetime.

In the same year, he began to record his dreams. Again, he anticipated modern ideas – this time of dream symbolism – and saw a relationship between objects appearing in dreams and their counterparts on another plane. Light represented intelligence; heaps of rags, gross thoughts; and soldiers marching past his window, protection from harm. This was the beginning of his 'science of correspondences', which was related to poetic imagery but transcended it. An unpublished dream journal for the year 1744 depicts the struggle between Swedenborg's dependence on scientific methods and his growing interest in spiritual conceptions.

In April 1744, Swedenborg's first psychic crisis occurred. In bed, Swedenborg heard a noise as of many winds, was seized with trembling, flung on his face by an unseen power, felt a hand pressing his own – which were clasped in prayer – and beheld Jesus, with whom he talked for a short while.

A year later came his most important crisis. One day, after his typically indulgent midday meal, the room suddenly darkened, and the horrified Swedenborg saw the floor crawling with snakes and frogs. A man suddenly appeared in the corner, startling him by calling: 'Eat not so much!' Thereafter, Swedenborg's life became very much more abstemious. That night, the man reappeared, saying he was the Lord God who had chosen Swedenborg to declare to Mankind the spiritual content of the Scriptures which He would reveal to him in due course. That same night, the world of spirits, and heaven and hell, were opened to Swedenborg. From then on, he forsook the writing of worldly literature to deal only with spiritual matters .

From 1744 onwards, he produced a stream of theological works culminating, in 1771, in his great systematized theology *True Christian Religion*. From 1745, he claimed to be able to live simultaneously in this world and the world of spirits. His first awareness of spirits was 'by a sensation of obscure sight' and a consciousness of being surrounded by them. Later, he seems to have seen and chatted with them at will, and as easily and naturally as with living people, learning at first hand the conditions of the afterlife. The spirits themselves called him 'the unaccountable one', because he was the only human able to live at once in both worlds. He was a unique medium: it was not the spirits who entered his world, but he who entered theirs.

Emanuel Swedenborg (1688-1772), left, the great Swedish philosopher and theologian, had many talents including devising new ways of using metal in engineering works, shown below and bottom, as well as a host of other inventions that showed him to have one of the most enquiring and incisive of minds of post-Renaissance times. His gifts were not entirely academic, however, for he was also one of the most convinced – and convincing – psychics on record.

He developed a variety of psychic gifts, including precognition and prophecy. On one occasion, for instance, he predicted the death of a certain Olofsohn at 4.45 p.m. the following day, and, on a journey, that his ship would arrive at Stockholm 'this day week at 2 o'clock' – an incredibly short time for the voyage. Both these prophecies were fulfilled to the minute. He was also an automatic writer and 'direct voice' medium, taking dictation from spirits, although he destroyed his scripts because his mission was 'only to tell such things as flowed from God Messiah mediately [in due course] and immediately'. His powers of clairvoyance became legendary. He once told a mill-owner, with whom he was having dinner, that he should go at once to his mill, where the man found that a large piece of cloth had caught fire. On another occasion, he told a certain Dr Rosen, who had denied owning a particular book, its exact position on a shelf in Rosen's attic where the mystic had never been.

On Saturday, 19 July 1759, Swedenborg was one of 16 guests of William Castel at his home in Göteborg, 240 miles (385 kilometres) from

Stockholm. At 6 p.m., he left the company for a time, returning pale and greatly agitated. He announced that he 'knew' clairvoyantly that a great fire was raging in Stockholm, that a friend's house had been destroyed and that his own was threatened. Two hours later, he reported that the fire had been extinguished three doors from his home.

The following day, Swedenborg told the provisional governor how the fire had started, how long it had lasted and how it had been quenched. A messenger from Stockholm arrived on Monday evening and a royal courier on Tuesday – both confirmed Swedenborg's account in full.

There are many such stories about Swedenborg's remarkable powers. In 1760, M. de Marteville, Dutch ambassador to Stockholm, died. A year later, a goldsmith sent his widow a bill for a silver service he had sold the ambassador. Convinced that the payment had already been made, Madame de Marteville requested Swedenborg to ask her dead husband about it. This he did a few days later, when he met the ambassador in the spirit world. The latter promised Swedenborg that 'he would go home that same evening and look after it.' It was only eight days after Madame de Marteville's interview with Swedenborg that her husband told her in a dream where the receipt lay.

SPIRIT CONTACT

Another famous incident occurred in October 1761. Augustus William of Prussia, brother of the Queen of Sweden, had died in 1758. The Queen, informed of Swedenborg's gifts, summoned him and asked him to undertake a mission to her dead brother. Three weeks later, the seer asked for a private audience with the Queen, whom he found playing cards. They retired into an apartment where Swedenborg told Her Majesty something confidential which he had sworn to keep private from everyone else. The Queen turned pale, tottered as if about to faint, and exclaimed: 'That is something which no one else could have told, except my brother!' When she emerged from her interview with Swedenborg, she was noticeably shaken.

On 17 July 1762, when Tsar Peter III of Russia was strangled in prison by conspirators, Swedenborg was at a party. A fellow guest noticed that, in the middle of the conversation, Swedenborg's expression changed and it was evident that 'his soul was no longer present in him and that something strange was taking place.' When Swedenborg came to himself, he described the Tsar's death at that very hour and urged the company to make notes of his pronouncements so that they might compare them with the announcement of the death when it appeared in the papers.

The Swedenborg Society headquarters in Bloomsbury, London, above right, house a comprehensive library of Swedenborg's works, besides holding regular lectures on his extraordinary range of theories and beliefs pertaining to both this world and the next.

The memorial plaques to Swedenborg, right, are in the Swedish church in central London. In 1908, Swedenborg's body was removed from London to Uppsala at the request of the Swedish government.

Swedenborg believed that heaven and hell are all around us, and that dying is simply the process by which our soul changes its state. The spirit newly arrived in the next world is received by angels and good spirits but, by a kind of spiritual gravitation, is drawn into association by inner similarities with those with whom it wishes to be, pursuing its own delights and ambitions and a life similar to its career in the body. God punishes no one, although evil lusts may be burned away and the damned tortured – yet only in the sense that they are restrained from doing the evil they crave. Every inhabitant of the three heavens and three hells that make up Swedenborg's spiritual cosmology, including angels and devils, was once a human being, for Mankind inhabits innumerable planets besides our own. According to Swedenborg, kindred spirits in the hereafter can marry; and there is no reincarnation.

What is to be made of a man with such convictions and eccentric claims? Contemporaries who knew him found him sane, sensible, of unimpeachable honesty, kind, generous, always agreeable, efficient in any work he undertook – but somewhat reserved. Jilted in his youth, he remained single, though attracted by women, and this has led to the suggestion that his experiences were due to frustrated sexuality. All one can say is that many contemporaries who knew him well accepted him, and the phenomena, as genuine.

PROPHECIES OF A HIGHLAND SEER

WHEN THE SEAFORTH FAMILY SENTENCED THEIR RESIDENT SEER TO DEATH, THEY ALSO CONDEMNED THEMSELVES. FOR, IN HIS FINAL UTTERANCE, THE PROPHET FORETOLD ONLY DOOM AND DESTRUCTION FOR THE SEAFORTH LINE

Popular faith in the prophecies of Kenneth Odhar, the most distinguished of Highland seers, was strong and widespread in the mid-17th century. Many of his predictions were well-known and were passed on from generation to generation. Some came true in his lifetime, others long after his death; but many remain unfulfilled.

Some of Odhar's prophecies may have been helped by his natural shrewdness. The sulphurous water of Strathpeffer, a few miles north of Brahan, for instance, had been shunned by locals as poisonous for years, but Odhar claimed that:

'Uninviting and disagreeable as it now is, with its thick crusted surface and unpleasant smell, the day will come when it shall be under lock and key, and crowds of pleasure and health seekers shall be seen thronging its portals, in their eagerness to get a draught of its waters.'

In 1818, Strathpeffer indeed became a fashionable spa; and the pump room, particularly, grew to be recognized as a centre for health cures.

His prediction of a disastrous flood 'from a loch above Beauly', which would destroy a village in its vicinity, also seemed at the time to be unlikely in the extreme. There was no loch anywhere near Beauly, which stands at the innermost point of Beauly Firth. However, in the 20th century, a dam was built across the river Conon at Torrachilty, a few miles away from Beauly; and, in 1966, it unexpectedly overflowed. The flood water killed hundreds of sheep and cattle, destroying grain, fences and buildings in the village of Conon Bridge, some 5 miles (8 kilometres) above Beauly.

Odhar's own end was, surprisingly, considering his gifts, unforeseen: but he did forecast with

Kenneth Odhar prophesied that one day the waters at Strathpeffer – sulphorous and unpleasant – would draw crowds of health-seekers. He was right for, in the late 18th century, it was discovered that the waters had healing properties, and in 1818 Strathpeffer was established as a fashionable spa. Its pump room is shown below right.

In 1966, heavy rain caused the hydro-electric dam at Torrachilty to overflow and this, in turn, caused the river Conon to burst its banks, as seen below. The flooding created havoc in the village of Conon Bridge, destroying buildings, crops and cattle. The precise nature of this disaster had been foreseen centuries before by the Brahan seer.

uncanny accuracy the end of his patron's line. Kenneth, third Earl of Seaforth, was a staunch Royalist who led a troop of his Mackenzie clansmen during the Civil War against Cromwell's army along the Scottish borders. Following the death of Charles I, he was imprisoned; but, after the Restoration, he became held in high esteem by Charles II, being granted extra lands and winning the hand of Isabella Mackenzie, sister of the Earl of Cromarty.

In the mid-1660s, the Earl was sent to Paris by King Charles, and several months passed without Isabella receiving a letter from him. So one night, Isabella asked the seer to tell her what her husband was doing. Odhar said that he saw him in a splendid room, well and happy, and 'indisposed' to return home yet. Isabella pressed him to tell her more, and the incautious prophet told her that the Earl was 'on his knees before a fair lady'.

The Countess immediately ordered the seer to be burned to death in a tar barrel as a witch. Odhar had expected a reward for his prophecies, not condemnation. But the Countess's decision was upheld and, attended by representatives of the Kirk, Odhar was taken to Chanonry Point on the Moray Firth for execution. There, he begged the ministers to write down what he was going to say.

When Kenneth, third Earl of Seaforth, left, patron of the Brahan seer, was abroad on business, his wife Isabella, below, having had no word from him, summoned the seer to Brahan castle – now in ruins, as below left – to give an account of her husband. The seer told her that he could see the Earl with another woman and Isabella was furious. Unfortunately for the seer, she directed all her anger against him, condemning Odhar to be burned as a witch.

Speaking in his native Gaelic, he said that he saw a Seaforth chief, the last of his house, who would be deaf and dumb. He would have four fair sons, all of whom he would follow to the tomb. One of them would die on the water. His daughter, whom the prophet described as 'white-hooded', would come from lands to the east to live at Brahan, and she would kill her sister. Thus, all the Seaforths would die. The seer continued: 'And as a sign by which it may be known that these things are coming to pass, there shall be four great lairds in the days of the last deaf and dumb Seaforth – Gairloch, Chisholm, Grant, and Raasay – of whom one shall be buck-toothed, another hare-lipped, another half-witted, and the fourth a stammerer.'

There would also be a laird of Tulloch, 'stag-like', who would kill four wives in succession, but the fifth would outlive him.

Odhar was executed near the modern Chanonry Point lighthouse, by the road from Fortrose to Fort George ferry; and, to this day, the place is marked with a stone slab. The memory and the implied threat of his predictions continued to live on – not least in the minds of the Seaforth family – long after Odhar's execution. For the next hundred years, their fortunes fluctuated, and several of them must have wondered if extinction could be close at hand. For their activities in the uprisings of 1715, the family were stripped of their titles, but these were restored in 1726, and the Seaforths subsequently became staunch Hanoverians, growing richer and more powerful in status by the year. The title of Earl of Seaforth died out with its holder in 1781, but the chieftainship passed to a second cousin of his – Francis Mackenzie – who seemed destined to bring even greater honours to Brahan.

Francis Humberstone Mackenzie was born in 1754 and, early in his life, became member of parliament for Ross and Lord Lieutenant of the county. During the revolutionary wars with France, he raised a regiment that subsequently became the Seaforth Highlanders; and, in 1797, he was created Baron Seaforth of Kintail. In 1800, he became Governor of Barbados, and in 1808 was promoted to Lieutenant-General of the army. As well as having military interests, Seaforth was an amateur painter of great talent, and he sponsored not only Sir Walter Scott, but also the painter Sir Thomas Lawrence, as well as the scientist Sir Humphry Davy in their early years. He was happily married to the niece of Lord Carysfort, who bore him four sons and six daughters. Altogether, he presented a picture of enduring, well-established worth.

But the truth was that the prophet's predictions had begun to come true for Seaforth when he was 12 years old. In that year, an outbreak of scarlet fever at his boarding school killed several of his fellow pupils and rendered Seaforth totally deaf. Over the years, his speech became affected; and towards the end of his life, he could communicate only by making signs or writing notes.

His eldest son, William Frederick, died as a baby in 1786; and eight years later, his second son, George, died at the age of six. His third son, Francis, a midshipman in the Royal Navy, was killed in his eighteenth year in a skirmish at sea – 'dying on the water', as Odhar had foretold, in November 1813. Finally, his last son, another William Frederick, the 24-year-old member of parliament for Ross, died suddenly in August 1814. Seaforth himself died in January of the following year and was buried with his ancestors at Fortrose Cathedral. His contemporaries and neighbours, as the *Edinburgh Daily Review* pointed out in an obituary, were the buck-toothed Sir Hector Mackenzie, the hare-lipped Chisholm, the retarded Laird Grant, and a stammering Macleod of Raasay. They also included Duncan Davidson, Laird of Tulloch, but it was to be many years before his part in the prophecy was fulfilled. When he died, Tulloch – then Lord

The stone, above, at Chanonry Point, Fortrose, commemorates the legend of Coinneach Odhar, better known as the Brahan seer. It was here that, in his final hour, the seer made his last prediction. 'I see far into the future', he said, 'and I read the doom of the race of my oppressor. The long-descended line of Seaforth will, ere many generations have passed, end in extinction and sorrow... ' More than a century later, the Seaforth line came to an end, just as the seer had foretold.

One of the seer's well-known proclamations concerned the depopulation of the Highlands, which began in the 18th century, when many tenant farmers were evicted to make way for sheep on the land. The cartoon, right, dates from the mid-19th century, when the problem was compounded by landowners charging high rents, forcing crofters to move south or, in many cases, even to emigrate.

Lieutenant of the county of Ross – had been married to five women, four of whom had died in childbirth. Between them, they had borne him 18 children, while his reputation for having another 30 illegitimate offspring in Tulloch gained him the nickname 'the stag'.

Odhar's final prophecy came true within a few years of Seaforth's death. His eldest surviving daughter, Mary, had married Admiral Sir Samuel Hood in 1804; and when Flood died at about the same time as Seaforth while commanding the East Indian station, Mary returned home in widow's weeds to take over her father's lands. This formal dress included a white hood – so that she was both 'hooded', as Odhar had said she would be, and 'Hood' by name. One day, she was driving her younger sister, the Hon. Caroline Mackenzie, through the woods by Brahan Castle when the ponies bolted and the carriage overturned. Lady Hood was merely bruised, but her sister died as a result of her injuries.

The prophecies of the Brahan seer form a perennial guessing game for those Highlanders who

know of them. Indeed, from time to time, they still appear to come true – as in the case of the Conon Bridge disaster. One of the most remarkable of the seer's predictions related to the emptying of the Highlands of crofters in order to breed sheep. This came to pass with the Highland clearances of the mid-18th century. But the seer went on to say that those Highlanders driven away to far-off lands as yet 'undiscovered or explored' would return to work in the Highlands in the days when the 'horrid black rains' should fall. Today, many Canadians, Texans and New Zealanders of Highland descent work in Scotland, notably in connection with offshore oil rigs, nuclear plants and submarine sites.

Naturally, the natives are curious: do the Brahan seer's 'black rains' – *siantan dubha* – refer to North Sea oil? Or do they perhaps refer to a fall-out of a much more sinister nature?

SUBUD'S EASTERN PROMISE

WHEN AN UNKNOWN JAVANESE BOOK-KEEPER, MUHAMMAD SUBUH, BEGAN TO EXPERIENCE VISIONARY REVELATIONS, LITTLE DID HE KNOW THAT ONE DAY HE WOULD INSPIRE THE GROWTH OF A WORLD-FAMOUS SPIRITUAL MOVEMENT

Muhammad Subuh, right, was an exponent of the spiritual discipline that he called Subud. Javanese by birth, Subuh received the revelations that led him to preach Subud while working as a book-keeper in his home town of Semarang, below.

In the early 1950s, a young Hungarian actress started to attend meetings of a group of followers of the mystic and teacher George Ivanovich Gurdjieff. She had become increasingly dissatisfied with the superficial nature of her life, and the Gurdjieff philosophy and psychological exercises practised at John Bennett's Institute for the Comparative Study of History, Philosophy and the Sciences, near London, seemed to her to offer the meaning she had been looking for in life.

The name of the actress was Eva Bartok. Sometime later, while in California, having just made a film there, she began to experience severe abdominal pain, and doctors told her she must have an immediate operation. Eva, however, felt impelled to return to London. She flew back, and arranged with a medical practitioner to be operated on as soon as possible. The doctors in London, however, told her something that the Californian doctors had missed: she was pregnant. Eva Bartok very much wanted to have a child, but she learnt that the proposed operation would be impossible without terminating the baby's life.

She was distraught, but nevertheless decided to go ahead with the operation. She was about to leave her hotel for the hospital when the telephone rang; it was John Bennett. He urged her to postpone the operation and go to his house at Kingston, just outside London, to meet someone whom the Gurdjieff group was expecting to arrive from Java within the next few days.

'He... is the one we are waiting for,' John Bennett told her. 'He... will lift our work to another level.'

Since Gurdjieff's death in 1949, the scattered groups that continued to practise his psychological exercises and physical movements had been without a co-ordinating guide. John Bennett, who ran the groups, had felt for some time that another teacher would appear – someone who would carry

Gurdjieff's work further. In his autobiography *Witness*, Bennett relates how, while he was on a visit to Damascus, Syria, in 1955, he met a holy man who told him: 'A Messenger is already on earth... Before long he will come to the West... you are one of those chosen to prepare the way.'

Now, a spiritual teacher from Indonesia was due to arrive at Bennett's Institute – a man known as Pak ('Mr') Subuh. Although to all outward appearances just an ordinary man, he was perhaps, Bennett told Eva Bartok, 'the man who knows where the switch is which floods the inner life of man with light.' Many sick people who had been in touch with Pak Subuh, Bennett said, had recovered their health, although he made no claims to be a faith healer.

Eva decided to postpone her operation for a week or so and went to stay at the Institute. Pak Subuh duly arrived in London with his wife and two disciples. Soon, his wife and a woman disciple visited Eva at the Institute and initiated her into the *latihan* – a form of practical spiritual training. A day or two later, she was taken to meet Pak Subuh himself. He told her that what he could teach her, *Subud* – the name was a contraction of three Sanskrit words, *Susila, Budhi* and *Dharma* – was not a philosophy, religion or method of faith healing. It was, rather, a practical process that awakens Man's higher centres, or levels of being.

Eva now began practising the *latihan* every day, and each day felt a little better. Then, one morning, she awoke with severe pains. Doctors were sent for, but it was Pak Subuh who arrived first. He came to Eva's room with his wife and disciples, and began the *latihan* with her.

In her book, *Worth Living For* – written, curiously, entirely in the third person – Eva describes how she 'felt shaken by a force that can only be compared, if it has to be, with electricity. It was frightening to her, and her whole body shook. It seemed to continue for a long time, blotting out all other sensations.'

The pain did not go away immediately. It continued for several days. Yet, slowly, she began to feel better. The day fixed for her operation arrived, but Eva decided to cancel it. Instead, Pak Subuh came to do the *latihan* with her once more. As she wrote: 'The same strong power within her shook her. She felt as if something new was born inside her and something else was dying.' It seemed to her that her old life had died and, with it, her illness. A new

The life of Eva Bartok, below, a Hungarian actress and follower of the Armenian mystic and teacher Gurdjieff was changed dramatically by Subud.

Eva Bartok began to live and, a few months later, she gave birth to a healthy baby daughter.

So who was this apparent miracle worker, Pak Subuh? Indonesian by birth, he had a remarkable spiritual history, according to John Bennett's description in his book *Subuh*. He was born in Semarang, Java, on 22 June 1901; and the month of his birth was, apparently, notable for the number of earth tremors recorded and the eruption of several Javanese volcanoes. At first, the baby was called Sukarno. The child was sickly and would not take food, and his parents feared he would die. An old man passing the house heard the women inside wailing and lamenting, and asked the reason. When he was told the child was dying, he said that he had been wrongly named, and should be called Muhammad Subuh (Subuh means 'dawn'). The name was changed; and, sure enough, the child began to thrive.

As a very young child, Muhammad Subuh showed considerable evidence of clairvoyant powers. When he was two, for instance, his grandmother took him to a betrothal ceremony. The infant declared that the couple were unsuitable for each other, and would separate within a year. When this prediction came true, the child's grandmother, not surprisingly, refused to take him to any more such occasions.

When he was about 16, Muhammad Subuh heard predictions, from more than one source, that he would die at an early age, either at 24 or 32. He left school and began to travel in search of a guru who would explain the reason for this. He sought out many of the spiritual teachers of Java, but every one refused to teach him. At last, one of them, the Sheikh Abdurrahman, who belonged to a Dervish order, told him that he would receive his teaching from a non-human source. Muhammad Subuh finally gave up his search, married, and settled down to life as a book-keeper in Semarang.

REVELATION AT NIGHT

One night in 1925, Subuh was out walking when he suddenly saw in the moonless sky overhead 'a bright ball of light... resembling the sun.' What happened next is described by Husein Rofé in his book *The Path of Subud*. The ball of light descended and 'touched his head and he began to quiver and shake as if attacked by ague'. Subuh thought he was having a heart attack, hurried home and went to bed. But a strange force raised him up to a standing position quite independently of his own will or intention, and impelled him to go through the ritual of the Muslim prayer.

This was the beginning of what Rofé described as a 'series of spiritual phenomena which lasted for approximately one thousand nights'. During this time, Subuh had many visions and inner experiences; and although he scarcely slept at night throughout this period, he was nevertheless able to carry out his job during the day. At the end of three years, the nightly visitations stopped; and for the next five years, he lived an ordinary life – its only curious aspect was that he noticed that his friends turned to him increasingly for advice and help, as if he had access to some special knowledge.

When he was 32, it was revealed to him that 'the wealth of power and illumination which had

been given to him... must be freely handed on to all who asked for aid.'

The year before, Subuh had already been told by an inner voice that he should now retire from all worldly activity. Accordingly, he gave up his job, even though he had a wife and six children to support. When his wife remonstrated with him, he told her: 'You will see that we shall be well provided for; we shall lack nothing essential.' He never worked for money again; and yet it appears that he and his family always had everything that they needed.

SPIRITUAL CURRENT

From 1933, Muhammad Subuh began to pass on to others the 'spiritual current' he had received. He discovered that it was enough for him to stand quietly in the presence of another person; within a few minutes, this person would begin to experience the working of an inner force. It was as if, said Husein Rofé, 'a new force was being made available in the world... as if mankind could now contain a form of electricity'.

But it was not only Muhammad Subuh who could pass the 'current' on. It seemed that disciples who had been initiated, and also had practised receiving the 'current' for some time, could then, in their turn, initiate others. The effects of the initiation might, apparently, include the healing of diseases, and the elimination of phobias and ingrained, self-destructive habits, such as addiction to drugs or alcohol. Although healing of long-standing illnesses had never been claimed as an end of Subud, it was often a by-product of initiation.

For a little more than 20 years, Subud spread slowly in Indonesia: then, in the mid-1950s, it began to move into the outside world. Husein Rofé was the first disciple to take Subud abroad – first to Cyprus, and then to England. John Bennett describes in *Witness* how he met Rofé in London in 1956, and was at first repelled by his presentation of Subud:

'He struck me as a man of unusual intelligence and very widely read, but his outlook was strangely materialistic... His stories of marvels, such as flights on the astral plane, of premonitions fulfilled and psychic phenomena, familiar to lovers of the occult, were anathema to me.'

Bennett was busy with many concerns at the time, and was also in the middle of writing a book. He told himself that he should stay away from Rofé and do nothing more about Subud until the book was finished. Then, to his surprise, 'the very same inner voice that I had learned to trust interrupted me and said: "On the contrary, you must go now."'

He went to Rofé on 25 November 1956 and asked him to perform the initiation that gave contact with the life force of the Subud *latihan*. Before performing the 'opening', Rofé described the force to Bennett as 'an electric current that can be switched on and off at will. He said that I would feel its presence as a thrill or vibration.' Afterwards, Bennett said that he had not experienced anything that could be called a vibration, but the restless movements of his thoughts ceased, and:

'I entered a state of consciousness that I had supposed to be attainable only by a long, well-directed effort. Soon I ceased to think at all, but

was aware of an almost unbroken consciousness, free from all mental activity and yet intensely alive and blissful.'

Bennett was deeply impressed. He went on practising the *latihan*, together with others in London whom Rofé had initiated. In February 1957, Rofé spoke to some of them about the possibility of Muhammad Subuh coming to England.

Pak Subuh arrived in London on 21 May 1957. John Bennett went to meet him at the airport, and saw him 'sitting quietly on a chair, alone and indifferent to the excited throng of passengers. Almost inevitably, Bennett saw in Subuh similarities with Gurdjieff:

'Both men had the same power to create around them their own environment, into which no alien influence could penetrate... Gurdjieff was... a striking and impressive figure... Pak Subuh was by

The Djamichunatra, above, is the name of the edifice built by J. G. Bennett at his house at Kingston, just outside London. According to Pak Subuh, the nine sides represented the nine spiritual powers of Mankind.

Indonesian shamans, as seen right, live in a society in which psychic powers are taken very seriously. Pak Subuh was similarly convinced of the genuineness of the spiritual instruction he received in visions.

comparison insignificant and seemed to deflect attention away from himself as if it were his will to remain unnoticed.'

A house had been rented for the little party in north London; and during the following month, Pak Subuh and his wife, with two disciples to help them, 'opened' more than 400 people. John Bennett described the process as follows:

'Subud acted with explosive violence. Many of those who came were either terrified or disgusted by the pitiless exposure of the human self, as it was stripped naked in the *latihan*... Others were lifted into such an ecstasy that they could scarcely be persuaded to restrict themselves to the two or three *latihans* a week that Pak Subuh prescribed.'

As to what exactly happened to people who experienced the *latihan*, Muhammad Subuh himself is quoted, in Robert Lyle's *Subud*, as saying that the

J. G. Bennett, right, was a follower of Gurdjieff who became the champion of Subud in England. In 1959, he organised a Subud international congress, below, at Kingston, near London. By then, knowledge of Subud had spread throughout the world – and the congress attracted over 400 delegates.

latihan consists of 'movements and vibrations felt throughout the body [that comprise] a process of purification'. This process, apparently, encourages each person 'to find himself... and become independent'. Elsewhere, in Gordon van Hien's *What is Subud?*, he is quoted as saying that there was no dogma in Subud, but only:

'A fact which works and grows and goes on by itself... our hearts change, our characters change, our physical health changes, and what was wrong in us is put right – all this is the working of a powerful force of life, which cannot be known by our ordinary instruments and organs of perception.'

With his customary energy, John Bennett threw himself into organizing and spreading knowledge of Subud. He gave lectures, travelled abroad, and himself initiated many people. Within four years, however, he had abandoned Subud – apparently feeling that it did not offer his restless mind enough material with which to work.

But the movement continued to spread; and although Muhammad Subuh died in 1987, over 10,000 people in more than 70 countries now practise the mysterious life-enhancing *latihan*.

*In*Focus

THE PRACTICE OF SUBUD

The central practice of Subud is the *latihan*, an Indonesian word meaning 'training' or 'exercise'. Novices are initiated into Subud with an 'opening'; this is an ordinary *latihan* which the novice attends with several helpers and during which the 'jiwa' (soul) is believed to make contact with the Great Life Force. Some novices experience visions or insights; others, peace or happiness.

The *latihan* itself takes place in a group and lasts about half-an-hour. Subud members will first remove their shoes, and then sit quietly for a while to free their minds from thought, desires and imagination. Slowly, they begin to experience a 'purification'; this may take the form of movement, such as walking around the room, dancing or physical exercises; sounds, such as singing, chanting or even shouting; or just being very quiet, perhaps lying down on the floor for the entire duration of the *latihan*.

The word 'Subud' denotes the harmony of Man's outer and inner life which will occur when he lives in accordance with the divine principle revealed to him through the practice of the spiritual exercise taking place during the *latihan*.

 SUBUD'S FUNCTION IS TO EFFECT A CLEANSING PROCESS, TO FREE MANKIND FROM THE INFLUENCE OF THE LOWER MATERIAL, AND OTHER FORCES WHICH AT PRESENT DOMINATE MOST PEOPLE, TO ENABLE MEN TO BE TRANSFORMED INTO NOBLE AND SPIRITUAL BEINGS.

J. P. BARTER,
TOWARDS SUBUD

EDGAR CAYCE – THE SLEEPING PROPHET

EVERY YEAR, LARGE NUMBERS OF PEOPLE ARE STILL CURED THROUGH THE WRITINGS OF A REMARKABLE AMERICAN PSYCHIC HEALER, EDGAR CAYCE, WHO DIED IN 1945

Unlike other psychic healers, whose very personal ways of curing die with them, Edgar Cayce left a legacy of treatments and remedies still in use decades after his death in 1945. Thousands of his 'readings' – the name given to the transcriptions of what he said in trance to diagnose illnesses and prescribe for their cure – are on file and available for study at the Association for Research and Enlightenment (ARE) at Virginia Beach, Virginia, USA. But Cayce was more than a healer: he was also a prophet, a clairvoyant and a theorist on the subjects of reincarnation and Atlantis. And his personal qualities of goodness and self-sacrifice made him beloved of his family and all who worked with him.

Cayce was born on a Kentucky farm on 18 March 1877. He was a loner as a child, and did so poorly at school that his parents despaired of him at first. Wanting to please them, he was delighted when a voice told him that help would come to him when he slept – if, that is, he promised to help the sick and afflicted. He then found that merely by sleeping with a schoolbook under his pillow, he could learn its entire contents. This made him a genius at the age of nine, but it did not help him adjust to school any better, and he left for good when he was 15 years old.

Around that time, Cayce was struck on the base of his spine by a baseball and suffered great pain. Lying for some time in a semi-daze, he suddenly ordered his mother to prepare and apply a poultice according to his directions, which she did some-

The portrait of Edgar Cayce – healer, clairvoyant and mystic – right, was taken at Virginia Beach, Virginia. USA, in 1941. Cayce had founded the Association for Research and Enlightenment, below, at Virginia Beach to further his work. More than 45 years after his death, the Association continues its research.

what reluctantly. The next morning, he was completely better.

The young Cayce worked as a sales assistant for the next few years. Then, after his marriage to Gertrude Evans, who later became his most trusted associate in his healing work, he took a job as a travelling insurance salesman. While on the road in 1900, he lost his voice and spent fruitless months searching for a cure, trying orthodox doctors, chiropractors, hypnotists – anyone, in fact, who might possibly have been able to help.

TRANCE CURES

In desperation about a year later, he agreed to consult a local amateur hypnotist, Al Layne. According to Layne, hypnotism had not previously worked on Cayce because he would not accept post-hypnotic suggestion. So Layne came up with the idea that Cayce should make the post-hypnotic suggestion to himself while still under hypnosis. It worked. Cayce was able to diagnose the source of his problem and cured it. He then cured Layne of a long-term ailment, again in trance. This led Layne to suggest that the two should work together to cure others, but Cayce was not happy with the idea. He refused, and immediately afterwards lost his voice. Taking this as a sign that his gift of healing was indeed from God, he now agreed to try to use it in the service of others. Thereafter, he found that if he stopped his readings, or if he used his gift of healing in any way contrary to his strong Christian tenets of right and wrong, he would either lose his voice or suffer severe headaches.

At first, Layne would hypnotise Cayce in the presence of those seeking his help. Later, however, Cayce would simply put himself into a trance and treat the sick from a distance. All that he needed was the name and address of the sick person. At the start of every reading, he was told: 'You have before you the body of [name and address]. You will go over this body carefully, noting its condition and any parts that are ailing. You will give the cause of such ailments and suggest treatments to bring about a cure.'

Cayce would reply in medical terms (of which he understood nothing when in the normal state). He

The young Edgar Cayce, above, discovered his talents as a healer when he cured himself of an illness by autosuggestion while in a hypnotic trance. Cures of other people's ailments soon followed. Cayce found, however, that he could use his gifts only for the good of other people: any attempt to reap a financial reward made him physically ill.

sometimes suggested orthodox surgery and drugs; sometimes, alternative methods such as osteopathy and a particular diet. But at times, the remedies were extraordinary, requiring ingredients and formulae that had to be searched out. For example, he once prescribed the use of balsam of sulphur, which no chemist had ever heard of. But it was finally found in a drug catalogue that was 50 years out of date. However extreme or simple the remedies he suggested, they were all transcribed and filed. Many have been analysed and, it is claimed, established as valid.

As a test of Cayce's psychic abilities, Layne once challenged a sceptical couple to keep a record of everything they did on a certain day in Paris, and then asked Cayce to give an account of their activities. The accounts tallied, but the incident made Cayce mistrust Layne and he decided to give up their partnership and work at something else, with the result that he again lost his voice.

Recognising that his destiny was indeed to heal others, but unable to earn a living at it because he would not charge, Cayce compromised by giving free 'readings' on Sundays only. This did not work for long, however, for an article in a Kentucky newspaper in 1903 brought him a torrent of requests for help. It began to interfere with his job as a photographer's assistant, and so he opened his own photography shop to enable him to work as and when he chose, and so devote more time to healing.

PSYCHIC SUCCESSES

Cayce sometimes used his other psychic abilities, too. He was asked, for instance, to solve a murder in Canada in 1906 by a local teacher who was interested in the case, and helped to lead the police to the murderer by discovering clairvoyantly the hiding place of the murder weapon. Through predicting the state of the stock and real estate markets, he also helped a client make a financial killing – but this brought on a splitting headache that underlined his conviction to use his gifts only for helping those in distress. However, against his psychic successes must be balanced a notable defeat. With other psychics, he failed utterly to throw any light on the kidnap and murder of the son of aviation hero Charles

*In*Focus

PAST LIFE CAREER GUIDANCE

The archives of the Association for Research and Enlightenment (ARE) in Virginia contain thousands of written accounts of the 'life readings' that Edgar Cayce conducted for his clients. Cayce came to believe in reincarnation, and part of his 'life reading' technique was to examine in some detail his patients' past lives and to apply the lessons that could be learned from them to the present. The results could sometimes be startling.

When Grover Jansen asked Cayce for a 'life reading' in 1939, for instance, he was a 19-year-old student who had yet to decide upon a career. Cayce's past life reading was to make up his mind for him. In a previous life, during the American Civil War, Cayce said, Jansen had worked as an

army agriculturalist – and, as a result, 'in the present . . . mountains and streams, the outdoors, all those activities which relate to physical prowess, have an innate, subtle influence upon the Entity [Jansen] in its choice of its dealings with others.'

In other lives, Jansen had lived in the Roman Empire during its period of great expansion – and before that, in ancient Egypt. Cayce's advice to Jansen was simple: 'In those fields of conservation whether it be of fishes in waters, birds of certain caliber, needs for food, or protection of certain portions of the land or timbers, or the better conservation of soil for certain seeds or crops – all these are the channels in which the Entity may find contentment and harmony.' On a purely practical level, Cayce advised that Jansen should try to aim for government work in the conservation of natural resources. He did so, eventually finding a satisfying career as a US Game Management Agent, responsible for enforcing fish and game regulations throughout an entire state.

Lindbergh, a story which made international headlines in 1932.

Cayce's predictions were numerous. Once, for instance, he attributed blame for a railway accident to a trusted and experienced employee, and prophesied that there would be another fatal accident if he were not dismissed. Cayce's prediction was fulfilled: and the vice-president, who had refused to dismiss the employee, was indeed killed in an accident. But, although he gave such accurate predictions, the 'sleeping prophet' did not fully trust his own prophetic powers. Precognitions, he said, were fallible because the future always depended on people's free will. But in foretelling geological changes in the world – which included an upheaval in North America's western region and the disappearance of most of Japan into the sea – Cayce argued that these prophecies would certainly come true, as they were not dependent on free will.

Edgar Cayce is seen above, with his wife, *centre, and secretary in court in New York, facing a charge of telling fortunes. The case was dismissed on a technicality.*

In 1909, Cayce began a long and close association with Dr Wesley Ketchum, a homoeopath with a practice in Hopkinsville, Kentucky, where Cayce lived at the time. Cayce diagnosed and prescribed; and Ketchum carried out the treatment. Enthusiastic about Cayce's many successes, Ketchum sent a report on him to the American Society of Clinical Research in Boston, Massachusetts, in the late summer of 1910. An article in the *New York Times* followed, and Cayce was catapulted to national fame. Overwhelmed with requests for help, he at last decided to charge a modest fee in order to devote himself entirely to healing. But Cayce was not capable of commercial success, as he himself accepted; and the hospital that grateful clients opened for him at Virginia Beach in 1927 had to close when the crash of 1929 brought financial ruin to his backers.

After Dr Ketchum left Kentucky, Cayce worked only with his wife Gertrude, who supported him lovingly and loyally through all the vicissitudes of their life. And his gifts developed further. It is claimed,

At Virginia Beach, above, *in 1928, Edgar Cayce visits the site of the hospital that was to bear his name. The building now serves as the headquarters of the Association for Research and Enlightenment.*

for example, that he could break into fluent Italian and Spanish when in trance and dealing with people of those nationalities.

An important widening of Cayce's horizons came when he was consulted by Arthur Lammers, a printer who was interested in mysticism and astrology. Lammers asked the entranced Cayce to read his horoscope, and Cayce's reply that Lammers had once been a monk seemed, to Lammers, to provide evidence of reincarnation. At first Cayce, who read through *The Bible* every year of his life, rejected any such ideas, but he was forced to reconsider and later came to reconcile the concept of reincarnation with his Christian beliefs.

When giving his 'life-readings', Cayce would suggest to clients treatments to heal sick minds and spirits as well as bodies. To start a 'life-reading', having entered a trance state, the psychic would be told by his wife: 'You have before you [name and date of birth]. You will give the relation of this Entity to the Universe and the universal forces, giving the conditions which are as personalities, latent and

Cayce attributed his esoteric knowledge to an ability to tap the so-called Akashic or universal records. He believed that the conscious mind is under the subjugation of the subconscious or 'soul mind', and can therefore gain information from other subconscious minds or from minds in the beyond. But human minds are fallible – which could account, perhaps, for some of Cayce's more extreme and fantastic theories.

Equally, it would be wrong to regard Cayce as infallible because of his well-documented successes in physical and mental healing. His biographies, all by admirers, tend to fall into this trap, offering somewhat specious excuses as to why he was ineffectual with, for example, the Lindbergh case. It would be equally unfair to judge Cayce by some of the sensational books about him, and from criticisms such as that of the 'professional' sceptic James Randi. In his article *'Edgar Cayce – the Slipping Prophet'*, a parody of Jess Stearn's biography *The Sleeping Prophet,* Randi rightly pulls no punches in demonstrating Cayce's failure in the Lindbergh case, but consistently ignores Cayce's many clairvoyant successes on record.

In judging the abilities of Cayce, two considerations have to be taken into account. One is that, so far as is known, nobody has ever questioned his integrity. Even if he was mistaken in his beliefs, those beliefs were certainly sincere and not those of a hypocrite. Financial advantage was never a motive for Cayce, and he remained poor for the greater part of his life. In the end, he exhausted himself and died as a result of giving too many readings for the distressed during the Second World War. The affection and respect expressed by people who knew and worked with him tell of an exceptional human being.

The second consideration is that he willingly and deliberately left the records of his life's work on file at the ARE, which was established in 1931. They are open to anyone who cares to look into them, and contain much by way of helpful remedies and suggested treatments, as well as accounts of the 'life-readings' he carried out for clients. Thus, the good he did has not been 'interred with his bones', but is still available to succeeding generations.

exhibited, in the present life; also the former appearances on the earth plane, giving time, place and name; and that in each life which built or retarded the Entity's development.'

UNFULFILLED DESTINIES

Some 2,500 of Cayce's 'life-readings' are filed at the ARE in Virginia. These, as we have seen, are based on the doctrine of reincarnation, attributing the deficiencies of those who consulted Cayce to failures to fulfil their destinies in former existences, and advising enquirers how they may fulfil themselves in the future. The ARE files also contain hundreds of letters from grateful patients who, by changing direction according to Cayce's advice, went on to fulfil themselves beyond their highest hopes. Sometimes, this happened in completely unexpected ways.

Cayce also came to believe that human beings were usually reincarnated in groups, appearing like shifts in a factory, and that those who were tied together by bonds of either love or hatred in previous lives were bound together – though perhaps in different relationships – in each of their succeeding existences.

Part of the Cayce archives at the Association for Research and Enlightenment are shown above. The files contain thousands of the 'life-readings' that Cayce carried out for his clients.

PERSPECTIVES

CAYCE'S OTHER LIVES

Among the 2,500 'life-readings' that Edgar Cayce gave, a number were devoted to his own past lives, revealing five highly colourful incarnations that went back to ancient Egypt. In the earliest, Cayce claimed to have been an Egyptian high priest named Ra-Ta, married to the incarnation of his modern wife, Gertrude, who was herself a high priestess. As Lucius, Cayce said he had been a relative of the Apostle Luke. In medieval times, Cayce was a Persian doctor; and, in another reincarnation, an Arab chief and mystic called Uhjltd, who went without food or water for several days in the desert.

Perhaps Cayce's most adventurous incarnation was as John Bainbridge, a gambling Cornishman, born in 1742, who served as a British soldier before the War of Independence. Ranging from Florida up to the Canadian border, he became involved in many skirmishes with the Indians, one of which led to his

death. It occurred while he was fleeing Fort Dearborn – the site of present-day Chicago, Illinois – which had been overrun by attacking Indians. Bainbridge managed to help a small group to escape the burning fort on a raft, but the Indians pursued them and wiped out most of the band. Those who survived died of cold and hunger. Bainbridge himself drowned while helping a young woman to safety. Strangely enough, this woman turned out to be the incarnation of Mae Gimbert StClair, a woman who worked for Cayce as a researcher and receptionist at his Association for Research and Enlightenment at Virginia Beach.

In keeping with his belief that former lives have an influence on present existence, Cayce realized that his role of healer was intended to make amends for those incarnations – such as that of the high priest Ra-Ta – in which he led an arrogant, materialistic and sensually abandoned life.

THE UNKNOWN PROPHET

IN 1914, AN UNIDENTIFIED FRENCHMAN WAS CAPTURED BY GERMAN FORCES. DURING QUESTIONING, THE MAN MADE A NUMBER OF QUITE EXTRAORDINARY PROPHECIES

Andreas Rill, a carpenter from Untermühlhausen on active service in Alsace, wrote two letters to his family in Bavaria, Germany, in August 1914. In these letters, he told how he and another soldier had captured a Frenchman who proved to be a somewhat unusual prisoner. After the man had been taken prisoner, he was questioned all through the night; and during the questioning, he began to speak about the future of the war. In his first letter, Rill wrote that the Frenchman was a 'strange holy man who said incredible things. If we knew what would happen during the years to come, we would throw away

Andreas Rill, a Bavarian carpenter, above left, sent home some letters while on active service in Alsace that were more than a little out of the ordinary. In one of them, left, he told of a French prisoner who had been able to tell him the course that the war was to take.

Andreas Rill's second letter contains details of the predictions of the end of this war. 'The man and his sign will disappear,' he was told, and hatred and envy would be rife. 'When there is a 4 and 5 in the year [1945], Germany will be pressed from all sides and totally plundered and destroyed.' Foreign powers would then occupy Germany. But, by virtue of its resourcefulness, Germany would recover. In the first letter, Andreas Rill noted further that: 'Italy will be against us in this war within a year and will be on our side in the second war'.

It was also said that many German soldiers would die in Italy. The letters tell, too, of a third war beginning with an invasion by Russia of south-east Germany. This was to happen during 1947 or 1948. During the war that was to follow, the 'mountains will spit fire'. Between the Danube and the Inn, it was said, 'everything will be totally erased'. The prophecy then continued: 'the streams are so shallow that no bridges will be needed to pass'. In Russia, the Frenchman said, the rulers would be killed; and there would be so many dead people that there would be no one to bury them.

SUSPICION OF AUTHENTICITY

At first sight, the letters are astonishing. The details in them are extraordinarily accurate, even down to dates. It is not surprising, therefore, that when they were presented for examination to the Freiburg Institute for Border Areas of Psychology and Mental Hygiene, the first reaction was suspicion as to the authenticity of the letters. But experts in criminology testified that there are no signs that the letters are forged, nor that parts of them were altered after they were written.

After the first predictions had proved to be accurate, Andreas Rill told the story of the strange Frenchman to several of his friends in local pubs. Reportedly, Rill became almost blasé, and somewhat fatalistic, after he saw one prediction after another fulfilled: the German defeat in the First World War, inflation and, finally, the upsurge of Nazism under Hitler. Soon, the prophecies of the unidentified French prisoner became widely known

 THEN THE CARPENTER REPORTED WHAT THEIR UNUSUAL PRISONER TOLD THEM: THAT THE WAR WAS GOING TO LAST FOR FIVE YEARS AND GERMANY WAS GOING TO LOSE IT; AFTER WHICH THERE WOULD BE A REVOLUTION. EVERYONE WOULD BECOME A MILLIONAIRE; AND THERE WOULD BE SO MUCH MONEY THAT IT WOULD BE THROWN OUT OF WINDOWS; BUT NO ONE WOULD **BOTHER TO PICK IT UP.**

Dr Hans Bender, seen left, in the photograph above, is seen examining the Rill letters with Father Frumentius Renner. Father Renner came across these letters in the 1950s, and published them in a mission journal. Unaccountably, they passed almost unnoticed.

According to Rill, the unknown Frenchman not only predicted the course of the First World War, but also forecast the rise to power of Hitler, right.

our weapons today.' Then the carpenter reported what their unusual prisoner told them: that the war was going to last for five years and Germany was going to lose it; after which there would be a revolution. Everyone would become a millionaire; and there would be so much money that it would be thrown out of windows; but no one would bother to pick it up. (Here, the author of the letter remarked: 'Ridiculous!')

At this time, the prisoner continued, the Antichrist would be born: he would be a tyrant, passing new laws every day; and the people would soon become poorer without realising it. This time would begin around 1932 and would last for nine years. In 1938, preparations for war would begin – a war that would last three years, ending badly for the dictator and his followers. The people would rise against him in anger; things would become known 'that are simply inhuman'; everyone would be very poor; and Germany would be torn apart.

It was to the monastery at Sigolsheim, Alsace, above, that the search for the identity of the mysterious French prophet eventually led. Research revealed that a Frater Laicus Tertiarius – a person who lives in a monastery as a guest of the religious community – had died at Sigolsheim in 1917. Rill had captured the French prophet in 1914. Later, in 1918, when his company was stationed at Turckheim – indicated on the map, left – Rill apparently walked to a monastery to look for the visionary, but was told he had died. Turckheim is within walking distance of Sigolsheim. Could the French prophet therefore have been the unknown Frater Laicus Tertiarius?

in Bavaria, and one day a police crime squad showed up at the Rill's home to question him about his conviction that the future would bring tyranny. According to his son, Siegmund, it was only by chance that his father escaped imprisonment in a concentration camp.

During the 1950s, the letters came into the possession of Father Frumentius Renner, who published them in a mission journal, where they passed almost unnoticed. No efforts were made to examine their authenticity, nor to establish the true identity of the mysterious prophet. It was a comparatively easy matter, at the Freiburg Institute, to have the letters checked by criminologists, but it was the work of some years to uncover the visionary.

Through careful tracing of members of the Rill family and a minute analysis of the war journal of the company with which Andreas Rill had served, Professor Hans Bender and Elmar Gruber tried to find the exact spot at which the Frenchman had been captured. Andreas Rill's sons revealed that the visionary was apparently a rich man who gave away all his earthly wealth to join a monastery in Alsace. Before that, he was said to have belonged

to a Freemasons' Lodge in Colmar. Researches revealed that Rill's company must have been around Colmar in Alsace when the prophet was interviewed, and Siegmund Rill was indeed certain that his father met the visionary in a Capuchin monastery at Sigolsheim, six miles (10 kilometres) from Colmar, at the time. Some years later, in 1918, Rill and his company were stationed at Turckheim, near Colmar. Rill took the opportunity to go, on foot, to the monastery to look again for the visionary, but was told that he had died.

Checked lists of inhabitants of all the Capuchin monasteries in the area have provided one slight clue that might point towards the unknown prophet. In the Sigolsheim monastery, there had lived a certain Frater Laicus Tertiarius who had died at some time after 1917 but before Rill's second visit to the place. A Frater Laicus Tertiarius is a person who is not a member of a monastery, but who is permitted to live there as a guest. It could well have been that the prophet would not have been immediately accepted as a member of the monastery, particularly if he had been a rich man and a Freemason in his earlier life.

There are also several passages in the war journal that might have a bearing on the prophecies. One prediction the Frenchman made – noted in one of the Rill letters – was that a certain Corporal G., who ridiculed the visionary, would not come home from the war and that his body would not be buried, but would be eaten by ravens.

True enough, on 23 September 1914, Corporal G. did go missing while on a patrol, and the war journal notes that his remains were found and identified in February 1915. There is also a note, concerning Corporal G. and dated the day of his disappearance, from the private journal of Colonel Schleicher, putting it on record that Corporal G. was 'seeing spirits again.'

But why did such detailed and important prophecies not become better known? Why should the Frenchman tell his visions only to his German captors? Were these the only prophecies he ever uttered? And how reliable is Rill's evidence?

Andreas Rill's first letter is an account of what the Frenchman said, while the second represents

Rill's reflections on his experience with the visionary. The second letter, written some days after the first, also gives details about a third world war, and it seems that Rill selected from the prophet's words only those aspects of this prophecy that related to his home, Bavaria. In considering the predictions of the three wars, we should bear in mind that the prophet was French; and although the prophet is said to have spoken several languages (it is most probable that he spoke German with the soldiers), misunderstandings may have arisen through the prisoner's imperfect command of the German language. In any event, considering the Frenchman was interviewed for many hours at night, it is hard to believe that Rill could have remembered all he said.

❝ IT SEEMS SAFE TO CONCLUDE THAT THE FUTURE CAN BE AVAILABLE TO OUR UNDERSTANDING IN THE PRESENT. YET IF WE ACCEPT THIS STATEMENT WE COULD BY IMPLICATION, ACCEPT THAT PAST, PRESENT AND FUTURE (THE MAN-MADE CONVENIENCE-DIVISIONS OF TIME) EXIST SIMULTANEOUSLY. ❞

JOAN FORMAN, THE MASK OF TIME

Shown on this page are Warsaw Pact manoeuvres in Poland in 1981, above, and an anti-nuclear demonstration that also took place in 1981, in Bonn, then the capital of West Germany, right. The unknown French prophet had forecast a third world war that was to take place between 1946 and 1948. This did not, of course, happen. But could he perhaps have been 'tuning in' not to actual events in the future, but to the general climate of anxiety about the nuclear arms race following the atomic explosions that ended the Second World War?

Indeed, psychological studies have shown how poorly, in general, people are able to recollect events they have experienced. One should not forget, too, that the prisoner's prophecies were of the highest interest among the soldiers and that discussion may have prompted embroidery of the truth.

But the prophecies do, with astounding accuracy, forecast political developments in Europe for many years to come. They include the duration of the First World War from 1 August 1914 to the armistice of 11 November 1918; revolution and the establishment of the Weimar Republic on 9 November 1918; the leftist revolution and its failure to retain power; inflation until 1923; the election of the Nazi party in January 1933; the occupation of Czechoslovakia in March 1939; the attack on Poland in August 1939; the occupation of Norway and Holland in May 1940; the attack on Russia in June 1941; the landing of Allied forces in Sicily in July 1943; Hitler's suicide; the surrender of Germany in May 1945, and its occupation by American, English, French and Soviet troops; the loss of German territory and the division into two states; and the rapid recovery of the Federal Republic of Germany under Chancellor Adenauer.

And what of the predictions concerning a third world war? A psychic who gives an accurate prediction in one case may, of course, be totally wrong in another. The time when it was supposed to take place, 1946 to 1948, has passed. This may mean that the prediction is erroneous. But the dates may also

have been noted wrongly, or the French prophet, speaking German, may have given them incorrectly.

There is no question that a third world war, with its horrifying potential for destruction, has been felt as a constant imminent danger. The psychic may therefore have 'picked up' this general anxiety and mistaken it for the events actually happening.

Whatever the truth, the case of the anonymous French prophet remains a puzzling footnote in the extensive files of parapsychology.

TALKING WITH THE ANGELS

JOHN DEE WAS A RESPECTED ELIZABETHAN MATHEMATICIAN WHO HAD MORE THAN A SCHOLARLY INTEREST IN THE OCCULT. HE EVEN CLAIMED TO HAVE FOUND A WAY OF TALKING TO THE ANGELS AND USING THEIR SECRETS TO DEVELOP 'ENOCHIAN MAGIC'

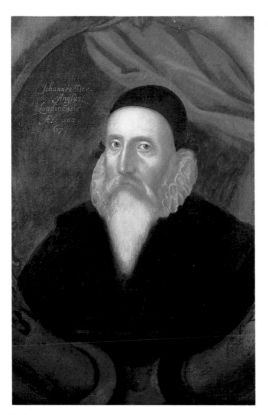

John ohn Dee rates an entry in most standard reference works for his contribution to 16th-century mathematical and navigational knowledge. Yet this same man believed he had learned the secrets of the angels – what goes on in heaven and which angels control various parts of the world, for example. So did he actually communicate with angelic spirits? Or was he the victim of self-delusion and the deception of a cunning medium?

The majority of those who have studied Dee's life and opinions have come to the latter conclusion. The *Biographica Britannica*, for instance, describes him as having been 'extremely credulous, extravagantly vain and a most deluded enthusiast'.

But occultists tend to take a very different view – particularly those inclined to what has been called the 'Western Esoteric Tradition'. This is a synthesis of European astrology, ritual magic, alchemy and other techniques of practical occultism as developed in the late 19th century by S.L. MacGregor Mathers and his associates of the Hermetic Order of the Golden Dawn. It also incorporates some of the principles of Dee's system of 'Enochian magic', based on his presumed mastery of the language of the angels, 'Enochian'. Some believe that Dee did indeed learn the angels' tongue, and therefore argue that Enochian magic is of great significance and value. Unlike other systems, it is not concerned with demons or devils, however; and, because the language is of heavenly origin, it is supposed to enable the magician to control spirits more successfully.

Whether Dee was wise or foolish, an obsessed eccentric or a magus, there can be no doubt of his dedication to scholarship. His library, the printed and manuscript contents of which cost him more than £3,000 (a huge amount at the time), was a

John Dee, left, was known as a scholar and the developer of an intriguing system of magic.

Dee's crystal ball, top left, was used by the mediums through whom he worked.

The wax talisman, top, was made by Edward Kelley, Dee's partner in magic, on directions he received from an angel.

The manuscript, above, was owned by Dee. It gives instructions for invoking Venus in ritual magic.

The next 30 years or so of Dee's life were eventful, exciting, and sometimes perilous. He travelled widely in Europe, lecturing at ancient universities and making friends among the scholars. He also became interested in the 'angelic magic', expounded by Abbot Trithemius in his influential manuscript *Steganographia;* and, in addition, he cast the horoscopes of many of the great men and women of his time.

It was this last activity that, in 1553, during the reign of 'Bloody Mary', brought Dee into danger.

At the time, Queen Mary's half-sister, the Princess Elizabeth, was being held in semi-confinement, since she was suspected of plotting with Protestant malcontents to overthrow the Queen and place herself on the throne. Through one of her ladies-in-waiting, Blanche Parry, the Princess entered into a correspondence with Dee, which eventually resulted in the astrologer showing her Queen Mary's horoscope.

Through the agency of two informers, the links between Dee and Elizabeth were conveyed to the Queen's council. Immediately, the unfortunate astrologer was arrested and thrown into prison. Not only were his astrological researches into the probable duration of Mary's life regarded as near treason, but it was believed likely that he was attempting to murder her by black magic.

Eventually, Dee was cleared of the charge of treason, but he was immediately rearrested on the charge of being a suspected heretic. He gained his final release in 1555.

In 1558, Mary died and Elizabeth came to the throne. Dee enjoyed Elizabeth's favour as her astrological adviser. Indeed, it was he who selected a propitious date for her coronation; and it was he who was called upon for advice when it was suspected that sorcery was being employed against the throne.

CONJUROR OF WICKED SPIRITS

Nevertheless, Dee's life was not entirely happy. He was perpetually short of money, spending most of his income on his library and alchemical experiments; and he was distressed by the continued suspicions of many that he was, to quote his own words, 'a companion of hellhounds, and a caller and conjuror of damned and wicked spirits.'

It is likely that those who regarded Dee in this light would have thought their worst suspicions confirmed if they had known of Dee's experiments in communication with the angels, which he is believed to have begun in October 1581.

The six months before this were troubled ones for Dee. His sleep was much disturbed, his dreams were peculiar, and there were mysterious knockings in his house. But as the Australian philologist and writer on Enochian magic Dr Donald Laycock remarked, it would seem that the spirits wished to contact Dee, rather than the other way round.

Dee worked through mediums, the first being Barnabas Saul who claimed to be able to see angels and other spirits in a magic crystal. But Dee was not satisfied with Saul and dismissed the seer after a few months.

On 8 March 1582, a new medium approached Dee – a certain Edward Kelley, a strange young man whose antecedents were obscure. He was only 27

very large one for the period, and it included works on every subject with which 16th-century scholars concerned themselves. Theology, mathematics, geography, navigation, alchemy, astronomy, astrology and ritual magic – all these areas of study were duly represented.

Dee was born on 13 July 1527 at Mortlake, now a London suburb, but then a pleasant Surrey village. In view of the importance he always attached to astrology, it is interesting to note that, at the hour of his birth, the Sun was in Cancer and the zodiacal sign of Sagittarius was on the horizon. This combination, according to astrological devotees, is favourable for a career based on scholarship and the study of secret sciences.

Such astrological indications were certainly confirmed when, at the age of 15, Dee became an undergraduate at Cambridge and commenced his studies with great intensity. As he himself recorded:

'I was so vehemently bent to studie, that for those years I did inviolably keep this order; only to sleepe four houres every night; to allow to meate and drinke (and some refreshing after) two houres every day; and of the other 18 houres all (except the times of going to and being at divine service) was spent in my studies and learning.'

Dee's efforts received their due reward: in 1546, he was appointed Greek under-reader, a sort of junior professor. He was also made a fellow of the newly founded Trinity College. But even at this early stage of his career, there were whispers that he dabbled in black magic. Some even suspected that an ingenious mechanical beetle, devised by him for use as a special effect in a Greek play, was a creature from hell.

MR

MARY

Dee: As concerning the vision which was presented yesternight (unlooked for) to the sight of Edward Kelley as he sat at supper with me, in my hall, I mean the appearing of the very sea, and many ships thereon, and the cutting of the head of a woman, by a tall black man, what are we to imagine thereof?

Uriel: The one did signify the provision of foreign powers against the welfare of this land: which they shall shortly put into practice. The other, the death of the Queen of Scots: it is not long unto it.

In other words, Uriel – speaking through Kelley in the year 1583 – was specifically prophesying an attempt at the invasion of England by some large fleet, and the execution of Mary Stuart, Queen of Scots. The reference to the executioner as a 'black man', meanwhile, may well have been an indication of the executioner in his black hood.

LANGUAGE OF EDEN

As it turned out, Mary was executed in 1587 and the attempted invasion by the Spanish Armada came in 1588. But little of the information supplied by the angels was as specific as this. Much of it consisted of obscure magical, mathematical and, particularly, linguistic teaching. The language of Enochian was, according to Uriel and his fellows, that originally spoken in the Garden of Eden. Lengthy discourses were dictated to Dee in this tongue – at first sight, gibberish. For instance, *micaolz olprt* means 'mighty light' and *bliors ds odo* means 'comfort which openest'. But sometimes, translations were obligingly provided by the angels. From these, it is clear that Enochian is more than mere strings of syllables. It exhibits traces of syntax and grammar, and has the rudiments of language.

The illustration, right, shows Kelley raising the dead in the churchyard of Walton-le-Dale in Lancashire. Kelley was a man of ill-repute with a shady past, but he won Dee's confidence on the basis of his psychic skills.

The manuscript, far right, is in Dee's own hand and records one of the conversations that took place with the angels.

Two of the most prominent women in Dee's life were Queen Mary, left, and Queen Elizabeth, below left. Mary imprisoned him for showing his horoscope of her to Princess Elizabeth who, when she ascended the throne, made him her astrological adviser.

The Spanish Armada, below, was sent against England in 1588. Five years before, Dee had learned about the invasion in a conversation with the angel Uriel who, as usual, communicated through Kelley.

years old, but his short life seems to have been full of mystery, danger and questionable deeds. He had been a student but had not taken a degree, becoming a notary instead. Accused of forgery in the course of his work, he was said to have had his ears cropped for his offence. He had also supposedly employed ritual magic in the search for buried treasure, had studied alchémy and was in possession of strange elixirs, powders and coded manuscripts. Most sinister of all, he was reputed to practise necromancy, the rite of raising the dead for the purposes of prediction and divination. At first, Dee was suspicious of Kelley, but not for long – for Kelley saw the angel Uriel in Dee's 'shewstone' and was given instructions for the manufacture of a powerful talisman. This convinced Dee of his magical powers.

The association between Dee and Kelley lasted seven years, and the two held hundreds of seances, the first at Mortlake, the last at Cracow in Poland. On the instructions of the angels who spoke through Kelley, the men and their families had wandered thousands of miles up and down Europe.

Records of many of their experiments, carefully compiled by Dee, have survived to the present day, but they are often virtually meaningless to the modern reader who has not made a specialised study of Elizabethan magic and alchemy. They do, however, contain passages that seem to be precognitive.

Take, for example, the following exchange that took place between Dee and the angel Uriel on 5 May 1583:

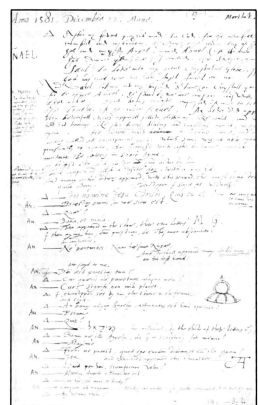

Dr Laycock has carried out a detailed study of Enochian and; in the introduction to his *Complete Enochian Dictionary,* he concludes that its structure and grammar are remarkably similar to those of English. In spite of his scepticism about the language, Dr Laycock is prepared to admit that there may be something in Enochian magic. Indeed, he has remarked:

'I have known well people who have pursued the study of Enochian from the point of view of practical occultism, and who claim that, whatever the origin of the system, it works as practical magic.'

The seance held on 17 April 1587 was the beginning of the end for the Dee-Kelley association. On that day, an angel, calling herself Madimi, gave instructions that the two men should sleep with each other's wives. Dee was deeply disturbed by this prospect, wondering whether it could be devils who were impersonating angels; but the spirits emphatically urged him on: '...In hesitating, you sin... All these things ... are permitted to you.' Dee still hesitated but, on 22 May, gave in and the wife-swapping finally took place.

This event finally placed too much of a strain on the Dee-Kelley relationship, however, and Dee returned to England, giving up all practice of magic. He died in abject poverty in 1608. Kelley preceded him in death, killed abroad in unknown circumstances, in 1595.

What then, of the value of the Enochian magic, the Enochian language, and the other occult teachings conveyed to Dee and Kelley by their supposed angels? No one can be quite sure. But there is a lot to be said for the point of view expressed by Laycock: 'If the true voice of God comes through the shewstone at all, it is certainly as through a glass darkly'.

A GREAT RUSSIAN MYSTIC

ONE OF THE GIANTS OF 19TH-CENTURY OCCULTISM WAS UNDOUBTEDLY MADAME BLAVATSKY, WHOSE 'PARANORMAL' FEATS WERE, HOWEVER, OFTEN HIGHLY SUSPECT

In 1850, the American painter A.L. Rawson, who was engaged in leisurely journeyings through the more picturesque countries of the Mediterranean, arrived in Cairo. He recorded that he was fascinated by the city, its permanent inhabitants and, most of all, the floating population of Bohemian cosmopolitans who had made it their temporary home. He was particularly intrigued by a certain Madame Blavatsky, who claimed to be a Russian princess, habitually dressed as an Arab, regularly smoked hashish, and took an active interest in the occult.

Madame Helena Petrovna Blavatsky is seen, above, in middle age. Unlike many women who have passed the first flush of youth, she often added a great many years to her real age, in an attempt to appear extraordinarily wise. She once told a doctor she was over 100, but in the end confessed to being just 53.

On one occasion, claimed Rawson, together with a friend, she visited Paulos Metamon, a Coptic (Egyptian Christian) magician, and asked him for instruction, saying: 'We are students who have heard of your great learning and skill in magic and wish to learn from you.' Paulos Metamon replied: 'I perceive that you are two Feringhees [Europeans] in disguise and I have no doubt that you are in search of knowledge. I look for money.' At this point, the interview came to an abrupt end.

There can be no certainty that Rawson's story was not invented. The 20-year-old Madame Blavatsky may indeed have been studying magic in Cairo, but she was undoubtedly a woman whose character was such that improbable stories were widely told about her.

She herself complained about such legends in a letter dated March 1875: 'There is not a day that some new story about me does not come out in the papers. Blavatsky was in Africa and went up with

Livingstone in a balloon. Blavatsky was in the Sandwich Islands and dined with the cannibal King. Blavatsky converted the Pope of Rome to Spiritualism; she predicted to the Emperor Napoleon III his forthcoming death; she cured the Queen of Spain's facial warts by means of Spiritualism – and so on... They say that I have spent several days at Salt Lake City, and have induced Brigham Young to renounce polygamy.'

It is symptomatic of the confusion and controversy that always surrounded Madame Blavatsky that more than one person believed that she herself was responsible for the dissemination of such remarkable stories. Nevertheless, it has to be admitted that the plain facts about Madame Blavatsky's life were quite as extraordinary as any invented legends about her.

She was born in the Ukraine in 1831, Helena Petrovna von Hahn, the daughter of a Russian army officer of German extraction. In 1849, she married General Blavatsky, the Vice-Governor of Erivan, but soon ran away to lead a wandering life – at first, according to her cousin Count Witte, as a bareback rider in a circus. Subsequently, she contracted a bigamous marriage with the opera singer Metrovitch, and there is reason to believe that she bore him a child. Her life with Metrovitch was interrupted by many quarrels and temporary estrangements. On one occasion, she left him to become an assistant to D.D. Home, undoubtedly the most remarkable Spiritualist medium of his time; and later, she contracted a trigamous marriage, this time to an anonymous Englishman, whom she rapidly deserted. But the marriage of Madame Blavatsky and Metrovitch ended in July 1871, when they were passengers on the steamship *Eumonia* which suffered a boiler explosion and then sank. Metrovitch perished; but Madame Blavatsky survived, having been picked up by a passing freighter and landed in Egypt.

Now a wandering medium, always poor, and continually hoping for the patronage of the wealthy, in 1873 she made her way to New York – wearing a red shirt, chainsmoking the cigarettes that she dextrously hand-rolled, sleeping in a hostel for 'working girls' and earning a precarious living by making artificial flowers.

Madame Blavatsky is seen with Colonel Henry S. Olcott, above. Both founded the Theosophical Society in New York for the propagation of occult and mystical studies. Olcott was a respected lawyer and writer whose interest in Spiritualism had led him to the Eddy brothers' Vermont farm. Here, he met Madame Blavatsky. From that moment, their lives were intertwined – although not, apparently, romantically nor sexually. An attorney, who had known Olcott well, said: 'He was as crazy as a loon on . . . Blavatskyism [but] her contemptuous treatment of him was humiliating to behold.'

Escape from this dreary existence came about through her acquaintance with Colonel Henry Olcott, a Spiritualist lawyer and journalist whom she first met at the Vermont farm of the Eddy brothers, the most famous of the many mediums who were active at the time. The occult wonders that took place at the farm were (if the accounts given by Madame Blavatsky, Colonel Olcott and many others can be believed) truly remarkable. Here, for example, Madame Blavatsky not only saw the spirit of her dead father materialise in a form so solid that she could actually touch him, but had a conversation with him in Russian, and was presented by him with a medal that she claimed had been buried with him in his grave. But the account she published of this was to lead to great controversy, for it was asserted that it was not in fact Russian practice to bury medals with a soldier's body and that Madame Blavatsky had invented the whole story as a way of publicising her own supposed mediumistic abilities.

Olcott, however, was greatly impressed by what he referred to as 'the spiritual miracles' he saw at the Vermont farm, and noted that they increased in number and dramatic appeal whenever Madame Blavatsky was present. He attributed this to what he believed were her mediumistic powers. She was, he considered, an altogether remarkable person; and he listened with fascination to tales of her occult adventures in Russia and Mongolia, hypnotised by what he described as her 'mystical blue eyes'. She, in turn, was attracted by his undoubted kindliness and generosity. He certainly gave her a good deal of financial support in the early years of their friendship, her exact needs being indicated to him by the spirit world, which regularly materialised instructional letters on to his desk or even into his pocket. Somehow, the Russian seeress was always about on these occasions; but Olcott's faith in his friend never wavered.

There followed another illegal marriage, this time to a young Armenian named Michael Bettanelly. Fortunately, the couple soon parted. Her

The alleged spirit photograph, right, shows Madame Blavatsky and an 'extra' (the face-like smudge, top left), and was taken in the 1870s in New York.

The Theosophical Society's headquarters at Adyar, India, are shown right. Madame Blavatsky and Olcott fled east after the publication of Isis Unveiled, which raised more questions – including that of plagiarism – than it answered. 'I want to go where no one will know my name,' she said. But, never a shrinking violet, she was soon a familiar figure, producing mysterious raps and apports at even the most respectable tea parties.

> BLAVATSKY'S THEORY OF
> THE COSMOS WAS THAT IT IS
> ETERNALLY BEING CREATED
> AND DESTROYED... THERE
> EXISTS... A UNIVERSAL OVERSOUL,
> FROM WHICH ALL INDIVIDUAL
> SOULS EMANATE, BEING
> ABSORBED INTO IT AT THE
> END OF THEIR CYCLE.
>
> **DAVID CHRISTIE-MURRAY,**
> **REINCARNATION: ANCIENT**
> **BELIEFS AND MODERN EVIDENCE**

A lantern slide satire, of about 1890, at the expense of the Theosophical Society, is shown above. Most of the allusions refer to alleged 'miracles' performed by Madame Blavatsky, or through her by one of her 'Masters', Koot Hoomi. 'Glass and china matched and riveted,' for example, refers to a broken cup that she mended paranormally. There was some reason to believe, however, that the repaired cup was merely substituted through her masterly sleight of hand.

husband's sexual habits, claimed the unhappy Madame Blavatsky, were quite insufferable – she had agreed to marry him, so she said, only after he had promised that there would be no physical relationship between them.

In any case, she claimed, it was not really she who had entered into the marriage, but an evil spirit that had temporarily possessed her.

BIRTH OF THEOSOPHY

On 7 September 1875, Olcott and Madame Blavatsky – or H.P.B. as her friends now called her – attended a lecture on the subject of the occult significance of the Egyptian pyramids. Olcott was fascinated, particularly by the lecturer's claims that spirits could be evoked to physical appearance by the use of geometrical formulae, and scribbled a note to his friend: 'Should not a society be established for the study of these things?' Only 13 days later, Madame Blavatsky was describing the new society to a correspondent:

'Olcott is now organising the Theosophical Society in New York. [The noun 'theosophy', literally meaning 'divine wisdom', was a 17th-century synonym for mystical religion. Blavatsky and Olcott's adoption of it for the Spiritualistic system they taught was totally unjustified and has led to much confusion.] It will be composed of learned occultists . . . and of passionate antiquaries and Egyptologists generally. We want to make an experimental comparison between Spiritualism and the magic of the ancients by following literally the instructions of the old Cabbalahs... I have for many years been studying Hermetic philosophy in theory and practice, and am every day coming to the conclusion that Spiritualism in its physical manifestations is nothing but . . . the astral, or starry, light of Paracelsus... '

The 'experimental comparisons' mentioned above were somewhat odd, to say the least. On one occasion, the early Theosophists applied a mild electric current to a cat, causing it to rise some way into the air. They decided that this proved that levitation was an electrical phenomenon and increased the power of the current, hoping that the animal would achieve complete weightlessness, but the poor cat suddenly expired.

With members engaging in such tomfoolery, it is not surprising that the infant Theosophical Society failed to attract new members and that, two years after its foundation, it had almost expired. It was restored to life, however, by the publication in 1877 of Madame Blavatsky's *Isis Unveiled*, a study of the occult that, so Olcott claimed, was inspired by astral visions. He wrote: 'Her pen would be flying... when she would suddenly stop, look into space with the vacant eye of the clairvoyant seer . . . and begin copying on her paper what she saw.'

BLAVATSKY UNVEILED

Whatever the source of the text of *Isis Unveiled*, there is no doubt that it is, at first sight, impressive. It gives the impression that its author was a woman of immense learning and wisdom, and the possessor of a secret knowledge known only to a few. But in reality, Madame Blavatsky's learning was not as profound as it sounds. W.E. Coleman, an American scholar, found that no less than 2,000 passages in *Isis Unveiled* were plagiarised from other books, and he argued that readers of the book had been misled into thinking its author was: '. . . possessed of vast erudition; while the fact is her reading was very limited, and her ignorance was profound in all branches of knowledge.'

In spite of the extent and verbosity of *Isis Unveiled* – Madame Blavatsky never used one word when she could use six, never wrote a sentence when she could write a paragraph – the basic doctrines taught in the book are simple enough.

First, it was asserted that the physical and mental phenomena of the Spiritualists' seance rooms, everything from table turning to raps and the materialisation of departed spirits, had all been known to the great philosophers and religious teachers of the ancient world. Many of these, so it was claimed, had themselves been powerful mediums, in touch with far more 'advanced spirits' than those contacted by modern Spiritualists. Through studying the lives and teachings of these ancient seers, it would become possible for 19th-century mediums to receive 'spiritual communications' of a higher nature than were normally available to them.

Secondly, it was stated that the old alchemical and magical treatises, seeming gibberish to modern readers, revealed under a veil of symbolism many scientific and spiritual truths of tremendous significance. Those possessing the 'keys' of initiated understanding – and the pages of *Isis Unveiled* strongly hinted that Madame Blavatsky was among them – could unlock the doors that would lead to a treasure house of wisdom, beauty and truth.

Thirdly, it was strongly suggested, although never openly stated, that Madame Blavatsky had been entrusted by some secret organisation of spiritual 'supermen' with the task of reviving the old spiritual truths and introducing them to the industrial world of the 19th century.

Isis Unveiled was a modest success and there was a revival of public interest in Madame Blavatsky and her Theosophical Society. Then, in the following year, D.D. Home published a book in

The Mahatma (Master) Koot Hoomi, above, *was one of the immortal 'supermen' who, Madame Blavatsky claimed, acted as mentor to those of advanced spiritual status, such as herself. Another was the Mahatma Morya,* left. *Her followers eagerly dispatched letters to these Masters – via Madame – and received replies that were oddly reminiscent of her own style and handwriting. But even so, the Mahatma letters persuaded many to become Theosophists. Among them was the journalist Sinnett,* below, *whose books* Esoteric Buddhism *and* The Occult World *rapidly became standard Theosophical texts.*

which he told a number of hostile and unpleasant stories about her. These proved so upsetting that Olcott and Madame Blavatsky decided to go to India: 'I want to go,' she wrote, 'where no one will know my name.'

In India, the Theosophical Society also met with considerable success, making many converts among both English expatriates and native Indians. The most important of the former was A.P. Sinnett, a well-known journalist, who was converted to Theosophy by a number of supposedly miraculous, but very probably fraudulent, phenomena produced by Madame Blavatsky – among them, the apport of a missing cup and saucer at a picnic. Supposedly, this had been magically precipitated by the Mahatmas (or Masters), immortal 'supermen', living in the Himalayas, whose pupil and servant Madame Blavatsky claimed to be.

Not surprisingly, some of the new Theosophists desired to be put in touch with the Mahatmas and to be accepted as their pupils. Sinnett decided to write them a letter, did so, and asked Madame Blavatsky to pass it on to them. A week or so later, he received a reply, which mysteriously appeared on his desk, from someone who claimed to be 'the Mahatma Koot Hoomi'. A lengthy exchange of

letters followed. Sinnett would write out his questions on a wide variety of occult subjects – the occult nature of the Moon, spiritual evolution, the nature of the Masters themselves, the lost continent of Atlantis, and so on – and send them (always via H.P.B.) to the Mahatmas. In due course, he would receive detailed replies.

On the basis of the information that was given in these letters, Sinnett wrote *Esoteric Buddhism,* a lengthy book outlining a complex occult system that involved spiritual evolution through reincarnation, a hierarchy of Masters, 'the secret government of the world', and a hidden wisdom available only to a few.

OCCULT WONDERS

Esoteric Buddhism and *The Occult World,* another book by Sinnett, that was largely concerned with 'miraculous' phenomena of the teacup variety, sold well and soon several branches of the Theosophical Society came into existence in England, France and other European countries.

Then, in 1884, Blavatsky and Olcott journeyed to Europe to visit their new disciples. In London, they called upon the Society for Psychical Research (SPR) and, along with Indian Theosophists, gave evidence of the occult wonders they had witnessed. As a result, the SPR decided to send out an investigator to India and prepare a report about the nature of the miracles.

The report, when it came, was devastating. The 'miracles', it was asserted, were fraudulent, the product of clever conjuring tricks skilfully performed by Madame Blavatsky and some of her closest associates; and the Mahatma letters were said to have been forged by Madame Blavatsky, their mysterious 'precipitation' due to having been dropped through gaps in the ceiling rafters. As for Madame Blavatsky herself, the report was damning: 'We regard her neither as the mouthpiece of hidden seers, nor as a mere vulgar adventuress; we think she has achieved a title to permanent remembrance as one of the most accomplished, ingenious and interesting impostors of history.'

Madame Blavatsky spent most of the few remaining years of her life in England, lecturing to her still numerous followers, writing copious occult articles, essays, explanations and an enormous book, *The Secret Doctrine,* a treatise on, and elaboration of, the system outlined in Sinnett's *Esoteric Buddhism.* Her practices were criticised by many; yet, as we have seen, the society she founded has survived, and still flourishes. Indeed, there have been, and are, many thousands who have sought to come to a better understanding of the mysteries of existence through a study of Madame Blavatsky's extensive later writings.

Mrs Annie Besant, who became president of the Theosophical Society after Colonel Olcott's death in 1907, is seen right *with Jiddu Krishnamurti, whom she hailed as the Hindu Messiah. Mrs Besant made India her home and dedicated her life to a quite different concept of Theosophy from that taught by Madame Blavatsky. In 1927, she accompanied Krishnamurti on a long tour abroad. On their return to India, he announced: 'I have seen Buddha . . . I am Buddha.' In 1929, he resigned from the society, denying his 'Messiahship', but is still revered as a holy man, especially in the West.*

Mahatma Gandhi, left, *was heavily influenced by Theosophy, when a young lawyer and working in South Africa.*

> **"** EVERY CENTURY AN ATTEMPT IS BEING MADE TO SHOW THE WORLD THAT OCCULTISM IS NO VAIN SUPERSTITION. ONCE THE DOOR IS PERMITTED TO REMAIN A LITTLE AJAR, IT WILL BE OPENED WIDER WITH EVERY NEW CENTURY. THE TIMES ARE RIPE FOR A MORE SERIOUS KNOWLEDGE THAN HITHERTO PERMITTED, THOUGH STILL, EVEN NOW, VERY LIMITED. **"**
>
> **MADAME BLAVATSKY,**
> **THE SECRET DOCTRINE**